Endorsements

This book packs a heavy punch! Its strength lies in the narratives derived from volumes of archival material, primary and secondary sources. The language is accessible throughout and lyrical/poetic in many instances. The histories Burrowes conveys are beautifully interwoven, and he argues convincingly that prior to 1800 CE the area now known as Liberia was a by-product of broader political, economic, social and ecological developments

    -- **Dr. Robtel Neajai Paley**, author and assistant prof., International Social and Public Policy, London School of Economics and Political Science

For too long, Liberian history has been told from a Eurocentric perspective, marred by myths and tropes of "savages" and "uncivilized primitives." Burrowes breaks that stronghold and offers a much needed retelling, from a Liberian perspective. Most readers will be easily able to follow this well-researched and well-written narrative.

Burrowes places the history of the people who became Liberian within the broader context of the African continent and Atlantic world history. He demonstrates conclusively that Liberia's ancestors shared many underlying economic and cultural ties. They were also fully involved in making the world rather than being inert spectators.

This book is necessary for the continued reconstruction of the Liberian nation because the history it recovers is empowering. It should be required reading for all Liberians and students of Liberian history.

    -- **Dr. Elijah R. Zehyoue**, African History Fellow, Emory University, Atlanta, Georgia

Finally, ...a readable, yet thoroughly researched history of pre-nineteenth-century Liberia. Written with care, it is a reminder that Liberian history is at once unique and deeply embedded in rich and turbulent events that have occurred across West Africa and the wider world. This mosaic of histories gives us renewed insights into who Liberians are and can be.

    -- **Dr. Cassandra Mark-Thiesen**, Historian of Africa and the Globe

Copyright 2025

Carl Patrick Burrowes

Cover image: kola plant, salt in basket, and malagueta plant

Special discounts are available for schools, book clubs, family groups and organizations. Please email knowyourselfpress@icloud.com for more information.

Contents

What is History? 7

West Africa, 9000 - 2500 BCE 19

Way of the Ancestors 29

Salt, Kola & Malagueta, 410-1085 CE 45

Trade and Migrations, 700-1230 CE 61

Empires in the Sahel, 1230-1450 CE 73

World Turned Upside Down, 1462-1591 CE 85

Mane Fighters Attack the Coast, 1540-1563 CE 97

Quoja Invasion, 1620-1650 CE 109

Shift in the Coastal Trade, 1650-1681 CE 121

Slavery, Scarcity and Suspicions, 1700-1800 CE 135

Echoes of the Past in the Present 149

Maps

Map 1. Liberian languages and ethnic groups.. 14
Map 2. Africa showing rivers in the Green Sahara.. 22
Map 3. Migration of languages from the Green Sahara..................................... 25
Map 4. Mask Styles.. 32
Map 5. Kru languages in Burkina Faso, Cote d'Ivoire and Liberia.................... 48
Map 6. Old trade routes in area of present-day Liberia..................................... 52
Map 7. West African trade routes c. 1000 CE.. 64
Map 8. Main West African Empires, 1000 - 1500 CE...................................... 74
Map 9. Spread of Manding languages in West Africa....................................... 86
Map 10. Mane invasion according to Andre Alvares de Almada....................... 93
Map 11. Nkérékoré and Musadugu area in Guinea... 104
Map 12. Quaja invasion as described by Olfelt Dapper................................... 106
Map 13. Major markets for Windward captives... 131
Map 14. Major shippers of Windward captives... 133

Preface

Who are you? To answer that question, you must know your past. That's because who you are shaped by all the things you have seen and done. No one should know you better than you know yourself.

Knowing your past is important for each person. It is also crucial for nations. Most countries do not allow others to write their history. Not the U.S. Not China. Not Rwanda. Not Ethiopia.

Liberia is a rare exception. Its history has been framed mainly by foreign writers who have pushed several false claims: That Liberian ancestors were isolated from the rest of the world; they were not. That they were "primitive;" they were not. That they were "devil worshippers;" they were not. That they were inferior to others; they were not. That they merely copied others; they did not. That local ethnic groups were static; they were not.

The Liberian students of foreign scholars have often repeated those claims uncritically. As a result, many Liberians mainly view their past as a source of shame.

Liberian Ancestors Before 1800 shatters those derogatory myths. It brings together oral histories collected in Liberia, Guinea and Sierra Leone. They are combined with stories recorded by Arab, Portuguese, Dutch, French, British and other writers. I spent over 30 years collecting written materials in Paris, London and across the U.S. All of those various strains paint a rich and complex picture.

As the world shifts rapidly, I hope more Liberians find inspiration in the example of our self-reliant ancestors as we forge a way forward. For individuals and nations, the path to a brighter future always begins with knowledge of the past!.

C. Patrick Burrowes

Acknowledgement

This book was written with the assistance of Dr. Susan Cooper, who served as curriculum designer (1981-1983), Ministry of Education, Liberia, and deputy director of research and development (1983-1986), University of Liberia. She prepared an early draft, located some of the images used in the book, carefully read my draft manuscript, and wrote a teacher's manual for classroom use by schools that adopt this text.

I offer heartfelt thanks to Dr. Robtel Neajai Pailey and Dr. Elijah Zehyoue, who took time from their own academic work to offer feedback on a draft of this book. Their insightful and detailed comments saved me from making many embarrassing errors.

Liberian Ancestors Before 1800 is published thanks to the generous backing of many supporters, including five who chose to remain anonymous..

At the level of Passing Grade, donors were Gledy Badio Wariebi,, Fatu Antoinette Togba-Mensah, Charles E. King, Matthew Toth, Gwendolyn Stevenson-Thiam, George Siaway, Emmanuel Woods, and Henrique Hopkins,

Honor Roll backers were Tanae Acolatse, Amani Emmanuel Jude, Cassandra Mark-Thiesen, Elaine Saba, Miatta Stella Herring, Ursula Brumskine-Bonar, Earl Burrowes, Bior Bropleh, Lucille N. Thompson, and Jeanine Milly-Cooper,

Salutatorian donors included Lydia Daniels, Karen Mygill, Marica Cox-Mitchell, Daiyouga Peabody, and Chris E. Dennis,

Valedictorian-level support was provided by Gerald & Roberta Cooper, James Elliott, and my wife Phemie Brumskine.

Thanks to Louis and the other hospitable baristas in Clarksville who kept me fueled during writing and editing sessions away from home.

Above all, my daughter Hyacinth provided continuous encouragement and invaluable business insights.

A **silk cotton tree**. These giant trees can live for hundreds of years. In African cultures, they are tied to longevity, history and the ancestors.

What is History?

Many people ask why we should study the past. They wonder if what Liberian ancestors did has any meaning for people living today. They claim that the lives of those in the past are so different that they cannot help us **understand** our own lives and the problems we face. Can we learn from history? The answer is yes, because knowing the past can help **bind** Liberians together as a nation.

History reveals what makes Liberians unique. As this book shows, both kola and malagueta spice were discovered by Liberian ancestors, who gifted those to the world. Also unique is the **snapping-finger** handshake. In addition, the Liberian identity is closely tied to the West African **forest**. Over several centuries, many groups seeking a better life or fleeing political, religious and other forms of **persecution** in the Sahel and the savannah areas found refuge in this forest.

But Liberians also share many things with other West Africans, including fufu and Jollof rice. People throughout the region pour libations to the ancestors and offer kola to strangers as a sign of hospitality. As do many Africans and their descendants in the Diaspora, Liberians fear Mami Wata and admonish children with stories of Spider the Trickster. Local ethnic groups have relatives in Sierra Leone, Guinea, Cote d'Ivoire and beyond. These deep cultural ties do not make sense without an understanding of history.

Thousands of years ago, the ancestors of West Africans lived together near the southern border of Algeria. That area was then green and lush. But the climate changed, which turned the region into a dry, brown desert. Unable to grow food or keep animals, West African ancestors moved south to the Sahel.

Over thousands of years, peoples from the Sahel gradually moved east, west and south into the forests of West Africa. Some Atlantic-language and Kru-language speakers entered the area now called Liberia first (see pp. 24-25, 41-53). Beginning in the 1200 CE, they were joined by Mande-language groups. After millions of Africans were taken into slavery in the Americas, some repatriated to the area in the 1800s, meaning they "returned to the land of their fathers" (See chart on p. 13).

As a result, the story of Liberian ancestors was shaped by **migrations**. But migrations are not unique to Liberians. It is universal. For example, the ancestors of most Americans today came from Europe or were brought there from Africa.

Europeans called the area composed of present-day Sierra Leone, Liberia, and Côte d'Ivoire by several names. Some called it the **Windward Coast** because of a steady sea breeze blowing from west to east. The area from Dakar to Cape Palmas was named the **Grain Coast** because local people grew a lot of rice. Still others labeled the area between River Cess and Cape Palmas as "the **Malagueta Coast**" because of a spice that grew in this area.

Local people sold malagueta as far north as the Sahel and ports on the Mediterranean Sea. From there, Arabs traded it in Europe and the Middle East. Later, the Portuguese and then the English carried the spice to Europe onboard their ships.

An African Perspective

Why is studying history important? Where do we get facts about past events and people? Do Africans and non-Africans view African history differently? If so, is it important for Africans to have an **African perspective** on the past? These are the questions

For more information, see these:

Amselle, Jean-Loup. "Anthropology and historicity," **History and Theory**, Vol. 32, No. 4 (Dec. 1993): 12-31.

Blench, R. Archeology, **Language, and the African Past** (Lanham: Rowman Altamira, 2006).

Courlander, Harold. A Treasury of African Folklore (New York: Crown Publishers, 1975).

Drake, St. Clair. **Black Folks Here and There** (Los Angeles: Center for Afro-American Studies, University of California, Los Angeles, 1998).

Ehret, Christopher. T**he Civilizations of Africa: A History to 1800** (Charlottesville: University of Virginia Press, 2002).

Gray, J. R. "Dating the African past" (pp. 41-46), in J. D. Fage and R. A. Oliver, eds., **Papers in African Prehistory** (London: Cambridge University Press, 1974)

Nurse, Derek. "The contribution of linguistics to the study of history in Africa," **Journal of African History** 38 (1997).

Rowlands, Michael. "The unity of Africa" (pp. 39-54), in David O'Connor and Andrew Reid, eds., **Ancient Egypt in Africa** (Walnut Creek, Calif.: Left Coast Press, 2003).

Skinner, Elliott P. "The African presence: In defense of Africanity," in William G. Martin and Michael O. West, **Out of One, Many Africas** (Urbana: University of Illinois Press, 1999).

Vansina, Jan. **Oral Tradition as History** (Madison,Wisconsin: University of Wisconsin Press, 1985).

Wolf, Eric R. **Europe and the People Without History** (Berkeley: University of California Press, 1982).

Wright, Donald R. "'What do you mean there were no tribes in Africa?': Thoughts on boundaries and related matters in precolonial Africa," **History in Africa**, Vol. 26 (1999): 419-426.

that writers of African history think about. You should too.

History is the study of people and events in the past. Historians use oral traditions, artifacts, and written documents left behind by Liberian ancestors or people who met them to tell their story. However, history is more than just relating the past. History tries to **explain the past**, to find a **meaning** for events that happened. It includes more than just dates, facts, battles fought, timelines, names of rulers, heroes and villains.

History informs us by giving us facts about past events. It tells us how the ancestors lived, where they came from, and how they got here. History tells us of their legacy; it tells us who they were and what were their accomplishments. This gives their descendants **pride** in their past and in themselves. History allows us to recognize, honor and respect worthy people who came before us.

Yet, there is more to history. Studying the past helps us to understand who we are. From history, we learn that Liberian ancestors faced hardships, but they found ways to **overcome** them. Through studying the past, we learn how the past has **shaped** our present beliefs, values, and traditions. We get an understanding of why some of them have remained the same while others have **changed**. Therefore, history is important as it helps us to understand the present. If we learn from history, we can have a clearer **understanding** of the problems we face. But, if we ignore history, we will not understand how to fix current problems.

History is not static; it is ever changing. As historians learn new facts, they have to re-evaluate what they know and write new history texts. For example, historians have listened to oral traditions that were previously unrecorded. Those have changed what we know of our past. They have challenged historians to change what they write of the past.

History is both objective and subjective. That means it is both **factual** and filled with **feelings**. It is factual because it gives dates, events and facts that happened in the past. But historians, like the rest of us, have their own views, values and biases, which fill history with feelings and opinion.

Historians use oral traditions about past people and events that were remembered by some elders. In the past, West Africans memorized stories of the ancestors to pass down from generation to generation.

That is the subjective part of history. Historians influence the recording or writing of these events and facts. This means that two nations can have very different accounts of the past; it depends on their feeling about the event.

We must rely on evidence to write history, but we must make sure it is **reliable**. Americans wrote, and continue to write, many books on Liberian history. We must be aware that these books are written from their point of view. Some contain biases based on their values.

This means that some non-African authors of African history books, because of their biases, **distort** African history. Because of their prejudices, they come to conclusions about events or issues without looking at all the evidence. Some others may ignore evidence, force the conclusion to fit their **bias**, or offer assumptions without proof. The result is that many African histories are often centered on Western interpretations of Africa's history.

Early views of African History

Arabs were the first to establish trade relations with Africa beyond the Sahara after 700 CE when they invaded North Africa. One of their goals was to buy Africans so they could work and join their armies for no payment. To justify their involvement in slavery, Arab slave traders used selective Islamic ideas to portray Africans as **demons**. Popular literature and fairy tales, which depicted Africans in negative terms, were also used to justify this trade.

Europeans gained knowledge of Africa and its peoples from the Arabs. Their early knowledge of Africa was consequently tainted with **negative** assumptions about the character, history, and worth of blacks. Like the Arabs had done before. Europeans beginning in the 1400s CE bought African captives to use as slaves on a large scale. To justify further their involvement in slavery, many Europeans portrayed themselves as **saviors** of Africa while claiming that Africans were less than human. By the late 1800s, this idea was rooted in Western culture and scholarship, including historical writing. Africans were often depicted as **inferior** because of their black skin and tightly curled hair. The superior characteristics, they claimed, were the fair-skinned, straight-nose and straight-hair features of Europeans.

Negative images of Africans and their descendants abounded during the slave trade. Black men and women were depicted as **immature** children who needed to be controlled by foreign adults. They were portrayed as lazy, uneducated, savage, and superstitious. Africans were considered to be less than people. They needed to be enslaved to make them "***civilized***" and to protect non-Africans from harm. Western books on African history claimed Africans had little history that was noteworthy. Those texts advanced Europe's interpretation of Africa's history. They focused on what Europeans were doing to "benefit" and "improve" Africa.

Liberian Ancestors Before 1800

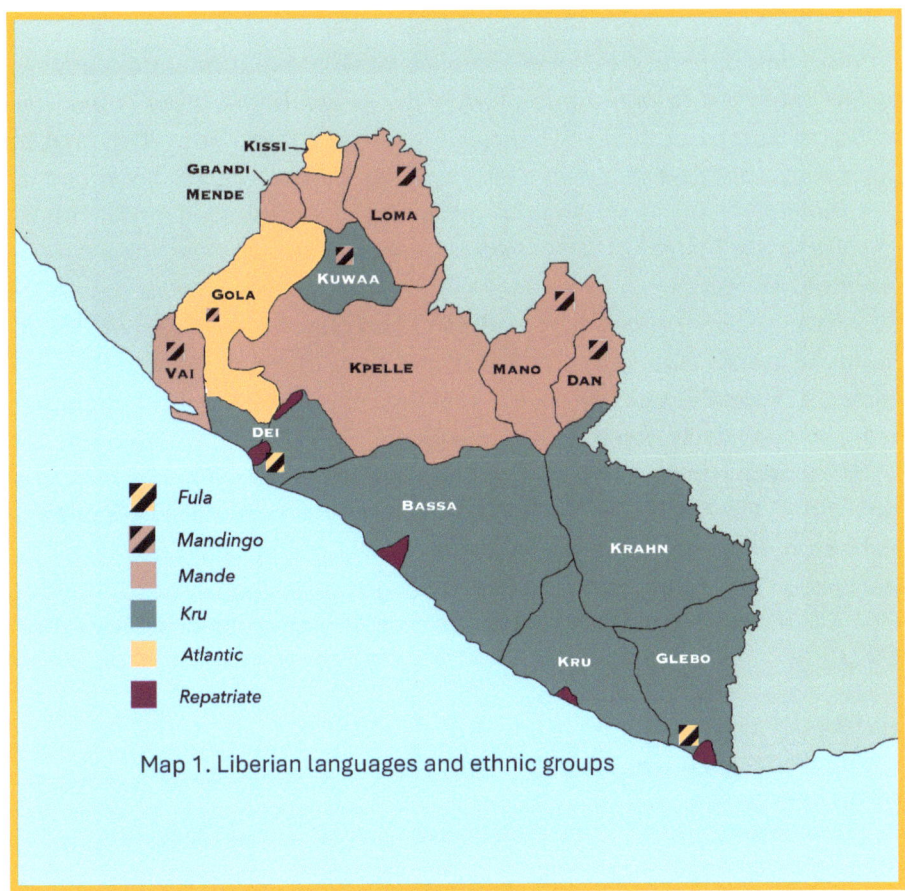

Map 1. Liberian languages and ethnic groups

Africans need to be aware of what information to include in books, what words to use and how to describe historical events. We have to use our own judgment and resources to portray history. This involves more than assembling multiple sources.

Historians must also ask **critical questions** about each source:

- Is it authentic?
- Is it original?
- Is it reliable?
- Is it typical?
- Who created it?
- When, where, and why was it created?

The goal of historians is to choose reliable sources, to read them reliably, and to put them together in ways that provide a **reliable narrative** about the past.

Sources of African History

Historians depend on original materials to write historical texts. Many historians have tried to write African history books exactly like those of the United States, Europe or China. But their histories have relied on written archival documents that have recorded deeds by kings, generals and ordinary people. Unfortunately, there is a shortage of written text to use in writing African history. The African historian must ask, how do we uncover the past when there is a lack of written sources?

African societies have a long tradition of oral tradition and few written accounts of events. History was told from memory. Many of those stories were framed as **morality tales** or tales of great feats, with members of one group being all-good while non-members were evil.

Many people believe that oral traditions are the only valid means of accessing the past. For African historians, however, history is more than just "stories" or oral history. It is documenting history from a wide range of sources, including oral history. These sources must be woven together. In short, there is no single source of material to uncover history. We must rely on different sources of evidence:

Traditional keepers of history, such as Jelis or **Griots**
Anthropologists
Archaeologists
Historians
Arab and European travelers

We have to be careful when using any source for a number of reasons.

As there is a lack of primary sources, many available sources only provide second-hand accounts. This means we often have few **eyewitness** reports of an event. We have memoirs and biographies written years after the person is dead. Sometimes oral interviews are recorded long after the event, when the memory of the event has faded. Often the recording of the memory was done by foreigners who might misunderstand the context. Sometimes the accounts are fragments that only tell part of the story. In some cases, the accounts are biased, giving us a distorted or slanted view of an event.

Despite the challenges, African historians use five main sources of evidence to write history: oral traditions, anthropology, archaeology, linguistics and written records.

Oral Tradition

Oral tradition is non-written history. In African societies, history, stories, folktales and religious beliefs are memorized and passed on from generation to generation. Because these are passed on verbally, the method is called oral **tradition**. Prior to the 1960s, African oral traditions were not carefully collected, preserved or used. Instead, they were widely discounted or dismissed as "myths" by Westerners and "educated" Africans.

But these stories are important as they often measure time in generations and provide lists of important figures. They focus on major **traumatic disruptions** like wars that are generally caused by "evil forces," some being invisible and magical. The stories tend to be mystical when they describe the origin of a group of people, their essence, or their reason for existence.

As with other sources, oral traditions have their **limitations**. In Liberia, they usually go back only three generations or so because most local cultures lack specialists charged with memorizing history. When groups move, later generations often mix up details told to them about a "homeland" they have never seen. In addition, "**praise singers**" sometimes change their tune to please current patrons, while downplaying or ignoring the good deeds of those who have fallen out of favor.

Archaeology

Archeologists spend their time digging up material and analyzing their findings. These materials are called **artifacts**. They include pottery, animal bones, the remains of houses, as well as tools for farming, fishing,

Where was a language born?

How do scholars trace the birthplace of a language?

First, they find the central block of closest relatives, which very likely constitute the heartland. Next, they try to match this place with known events that would likely have precipitated a migration. To find such occurrences, they study oral traditions, climate changes, and other evidence.

By this method, linguists have traced the roots of the Niger-Congo languages to the Sahara.

hunting and warfare. For instance, artifacts help us understand what people in earlier times wore, what foods they grew and ate, what animals they bred, what weapons they used to hunt and fight their enemies, and what homes they lived in. Archeologists contribute to history by finding out the age, function, and purpose of artifacts.

Anthropology

Anthropology is the study of culture. It focuses on how people live, organize, govern, create meaning to their lives, and adapt to their environment. Based on their work, the government of Liberia has recognized sixteen local ethnic groups.

Anthropologists sometimes

spend years studying a particular group. Their goal is to understand each **culture** deeply. Like other scholars, they are expected to control their biases from influencing their conclusions.

But anthropologists caused a problem for the study of Liberia. They imposed the idea of "**tribes**." That word is used to describe African and other people who are considered "**primitive**." Those groups are define themselves based on internal similarities of language, culture and descent. Like Europeans and people in other parts of the world, they should be called **ethnic groups**, which is a neutral phrase, not negative.

Anthropologists in Liberia have often studied each ethnic group in **isolation**. But, ethnic groups intermarry and trade with each other. As a result, cultures change. For that reason, it is important to study how cultural traits are passed from one region or group to another.

Linguistics

Linguistics is the study of languages. It seeks to understand the **rules** and structure of each language. By comparing languages, it is possible to find words they share in common.

Linguists have grouped more than one thousand languages in Africa into four families or phyla: Khoisan, Nilo-Saharan, Afro-Asiatic, and **Niger-Congo**. According to them, all African languages spoken in Liberia belong to the Niger-Congo family.

Linguistics is helpful to historians because it looks at how languages start, change and sometimes **die**.

Written Records

There are few written documents on the area now known as Liberia from before the 1800s. But we can use the writings of Arabs who visited societies in the Sahel of West Africa. We can also use books of European sailors and traders who traveled to the West African coast. Those texts discuss events they witnessed or heard about. They can help support or disprove oral accounts.

The Story of Early Liberians

The history of the area now called Liberia is one of many migrations. Over many hundreds of years, people from the Sahara and Sahel gradually moved east, west and south into the forests of West Africa. As a result, the ethnic groups of present-day Liberia are not exclusive to Liberia. Many extend into neighboring countries.

By using oral traditions, anthropology, archaeology, and linguistics, we can uncover history from an **African viewpoint**. By combining those sources with documents from Arab and European traders and sailors, we can write a fuller history of Liberians before 1800.

Rock painting from Tassili n'Ajjer, Algeria, showing ancient West Africans from 6,000–4,000 B.C.E. Archeoologists named this image "**Running Horned Woman**." Many of their masks and decorations look similar to cultures in the region thousands of years later.

West Africa, 9000 - 2500 BCE

Where did Liberian ancestors originate? To answer that question, it helps to look beyond Liberia. Why? The people of West Africa have many things in common. According to linguists, West African languages all come from the same source. West African cultures also shared many features like round huts and tales about Spider the Trickster. We share these elements because we are children of common ancestors.

Archaeologists have collected bones and artifacts left by ancient people all over the world. The oldest artifacts they found were in East Africa and date from 1.5 million years ago. From there, ancient people spread to other lands. For that reason, they say that region is where humans began. Scientists say people around the world are all children of those early Africans.

Wherever those ancient people went, they settled by large bodies of water. Those places supplied water for people to drink, bathe and cook. In addition, plants grew better near rivers and lakes, and animals came there to drink. People also gathered food more easily from those places.

The Green Sahara

The first people who reached West Africa settled near Southern Algeria about 10,500 years ago (7,700 BCE). In that region, archaeologists have found the oldest graves and earliest artifacts in West Africa. When the ancestors of West Africans arrived, the area was savannah or grassland, so they could move around easily. It supported many plants and wild animals that people could eat because it had four rivers and several lakes. At that time, people did not live in the area now called Liberia because the forest was too thick.

In Southern Algeria, the first ancestors of West Africans laid the foundation for life. At first, they apparently fed themselves by hunting and collecting all their food from the wild. To clear trees, people first used tools made from stone.

Farming, Herding and Iron Smelting

Artifacts from around 8000 BCE show that West African ancestors came up with two big new ways of doing things that caused them and their children to live far better. They started farming and keeping animals like sheep, goats and cattle. That changed everything. They now could feed more people by growing their own food and raising animals. They were able to have more children, so their towns grew bigger.

When the southern Algeria area was wet, rivers and lakes in the Sahara valleys regularly flooded. They teemed with over 30 species of fish, some 6 feet long. The rivers that flowed from the mountains and hills kept the grassland fertile. They also supported abundant wildlife such as hippopotamus, elephants and antelope, as well as reptiles like tortoise and crocodiles. With abundant fish, plants and animals, people had plenty to eat.

Early West African ancestors in the north left behind more than 30,000 paintings, drawing and carvings on rocks and in caves. Places with lots of rock art include **Tichitt-Walata** in modern Mauritania, **Tassili N'Ajjer** in Algeria, the **Tibetsi** in Chad and Libya. Their rock art show farming and hunt-

For more information, see these:

Ehret, Christopher. "Africa in world history: The long, long view" (pp. 455-474), in Jerry H. Bentley, ed., *The Oxford Handbook of World History* (Oxford: Oxford University Press, 2013).

Fagan, Brian. *The Long Summer: How Climate Changed Civilization* (New York: Basic Books, 2004).

Gearon, Lamonn. *The Sahara: A Cultural History* (New York: Oxford University Press, 2011).

McIntosh, S. K. "Archaeology of Holocene West Africa, 12,000-1,000 BP" (pp. 11-32), in Emmanuel Kwame Akeyampong (ed.), *Themes in West Africa's History* (London: James Currey, 2006).

Newman, James L. T*he Peopling of Africa: A Geographic Interpretation* (New Haven: Yale University Press, 1995): 11-21.

Portéres, Roland. "Primary cradles of agriculture in the African continent" (pp. 43-58), in J. D. Fage and R. A. Oliver, eds., *Papers in African Prehistory* (London: Cambridge University Press, 1974).

Sutton, J. E. G. "The aquatic civilization of Middle Africa," *Journal of African History*, Vol. 15, No. 4 (1974): 527-546.

Westermann, D.; M. A. Bryan; and D. W. Arnott, *The Languages of West Africa* (London: Dawsons, 1970).

Williamson, Kay and Roger Blench, "Niger-Congo" (pp. 11-42), in B. Heine and D. Nurse, eds., *African Languages: An Introduction* (Cambridge: Cambridge University Press, 2000).

A Special Note About Time

Historians measure time back and forward from the year 0. Christians were the first to divide time that way between BC (Before Christ) and AD (After the Death of Christ).

Because many historians are not Christians, they changed the labels to avoid being partial to any religion. They replaced BC and AD with BCE (Before the Common Era) and CE (Common Era).

To show respect for Liberians of all religion, the second standard is used in this book.

ing with rocks, clubs and bows and arrows. Also on those rocks are pictures of people making tools, building houses, herding cows, fishing, making music, worshiping, and wearing masks while dancing.

Some paintings show women, dressed in fine clothes with fancy hairstyles, riding on oxen. Other rock art show various animals lived in the area that don't live there now. They include buffalo, elephants, giraffes, hippopotami, horses and rhinoceros.

Life in the Sahara

Archaeologists have uncovered many artifacts left behind by those early West Africans. Under the sand, they have found fish bones, animal skeletons and dried tree trunks. They have also discovered human bones alongside tools. These artifacts tell us that the earlier ancestors of West Africans thrived in the Sahara area before it turned to a desert.

In 2000 CE, archaeologists found an old cemetery in Gobero, Niger, with over 200 graves. It is the oldest known graveyard in all of Africa. It dates to before the Sahara turned to a desert. By analyzing artifacts from the graves and surrounding area, they identified two cultures: They called one culture Kiffian and the other Tenerian.

The Kiffian

Scientists conducted several tests on bones and other artifacts at Gobero. They learned several things about the Kiffians.
1. They lived on the shores of Lake Gobero between 7,700 BCE and 6,200 BCE.
2. The Kiffians were tall! The skeleton of both men and women were sometimes six feet long.
3. Most of their bones were never broken, which means they were peaceful, not warlike.
4. The Kiffians were expert hunters because scientists found the bones of large animals scattered near where they lived.
5. They had lived near a lake, which dried up, leaving behind the bones of fish and other water creatures.

6. They fished using harpoons and hooks carved from animal bone to catch lake fish, such as tilapia and catfish.
7. The Kiffians wrapped their dead in animal skins or placed them in baskets before burying them. That tells us they had tender feelings toward their loved ones and probably had ideas about an afterlife.

Around 6,200 BCE, the climate changed in the area where those ancestors lived. Every year, less and less rain fell. The rivers and lakes dried up. The region turned into a dry, brown and sandy desert. Around 6,200 BCE, the Kiffians left because the area became too arid to support life. The Sahara remained dry for a thousand years.

The Tenerians

Between 5200 BCE and 2500 BCE, the rains returned, rivers flowed, and lakes reappeared in the Sahara. Lake Gobero again provided water to sustain life. Another group of people moved into the Sahara and made their home along the shores of Lake Gobero. Archaeologists call them the Tenerians.

Unlike the Kaffians, they were slimmer and shorter. Their skeletons were around five feet six inches long. Alongside human bones, archeologists found shells from clams and bones from fish, wild African buffalo, antelopes, gazelles and domesticated cattle. Those artifacts show the Tenerians hunted, grew crops and kept livestock such as sheep and goats. They also fished in the rivers and lakes.

The Tenerians, too, showed tender feelings toward their dead. They buried their loved ones with arrowheads, beads and even animal bones. They decorated some graves with flowers. One grave contained skeletons of two very young

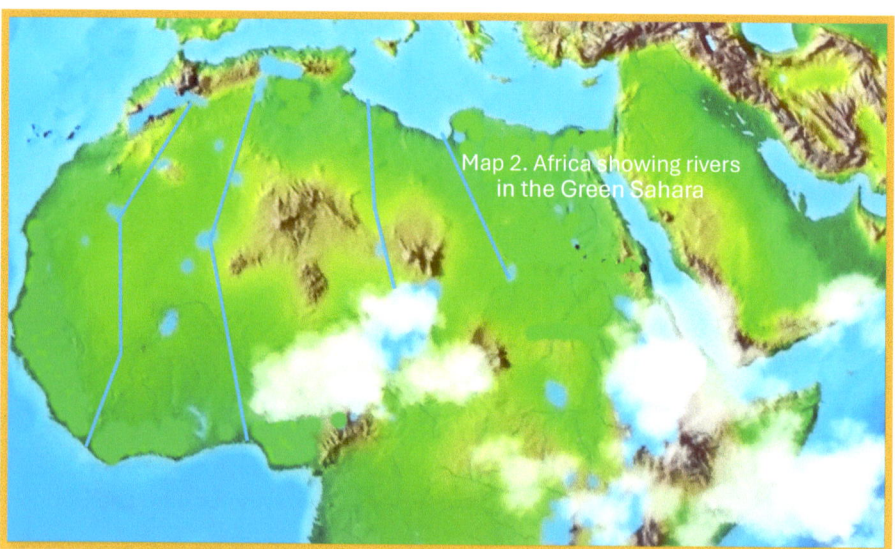
Map 2. Africa showing rivers in the Green Sahara

children and a woman. She was probably their mother because she was embracing them.

For as long as the rains kept falling in Gobero, plants grew, and animals came to the lake. People stayed because of the availability of food and water. But by 2,300 BCE, the Sahara was again dry. The lake again disappeared. The Tenerians abandoned Gobero, leaving behind their artifacts. They also left the remains of their dead ancestors, who they obviously loved.

Sharing a Common Language

Studies by linguists show that most African languages flow from one parent language. They may differ from each other in some ways. But linguists group them into one family called Niger-Congo. It started around Southern Algeria.

That language family extends from Senegal in the west to Kenya in the east and down to South Africa. West Africans below the Sahara today all speak Niger-Congo languages. Those languages share many similarities, and some even have common words and rules.

When the Sahara dried up, Niger-Congo language speakers moved south in search of water to survive. As they migrated, their common language broke into four branches in West Africa. Three of those branches are in Liberia: Atlantic, Kru and Mande.

Languages change over time as they pass from one generation to another. Languages in West Africa continue to change. On the one hand, some words from European languages have become part of local languages, including Liberian English, which is called Kolokwa.

Languages change for many reasons:

People may create words to describe things in their new location that did not exist in their previous home.

Strangers join local people may bring unfamiliar words and ideas.

Trading societies may borrow words and ideas from each other.

People invent words to describe new ways of doing things.

The Breakup of Niger-Congo Language

Before the Sahara became a desert, the ancestors of West Africans and those of the Nile valley lived near each other. One thing common to both groups is a hunting dog known as Basenji. It is fast, fretful-looking and does not bark. The dog appears on ancient Egyptian monuments with a bell around its neck. Because the dog doesn't bark, the ringing bell would tell people where the dog was.

The climate of the Green Sahara slowly changed, and the lake slowly dried up. The area turned to desert. Unable to grow food and keep animals, they moved, out of the Sahara-

Niger-Congo Language Families in Liberia				
Atlantic	Kru	Northern Mande	Southwest Mande	Southeast Mande
Fula	Bassa	Mandingo	Bandi	Dan
Gola	Dei	Vai	Kpelle	Ma
Kissi	Glebo		Loma	
	Klao		Mende	
	Krahn			
	Kuwaa			
	Sapo			

into the savanna grasslands of the Sahel. When no rains fell for hundreds of years, people faced hard choices. To avoid famine, some grazed animals at the desert's edge. Others moved east toward the Nile River or south. That shift in climate changed the history of West Africa.

Three areas in the savanna of West Africa became centers of farming, herding and iron working. One was northern Nigeria, the home of the Kwa speakers. Another was the Niger River, heartland of the Mande language group. The third was southern Mauritania, where the Atlantic languages began. (See Map 3.)

Today, some Basenji live among the Kpelle and Loma of Liberia, as well as in southern Sudan and northern Uganda. The dog's presence in locations thousands of miles apart is a clue. It suggests the Basenji was probably carried to those places by people who once lived near each other. In that case, the ancestors of the Loma and Kpelle brought the dog with them from their Niger-Congo homeland.

Northern Nigeria Area

Africans started smelting iron around 1,000 BCE in the area now known as the Central African Republic. From there, the innovation spread east to the Great Lakes region of East Africa and west toward northern Nigeria. By 200 BCE, people in the Nok area in Northern Nigeria were smelting large amounts of different metals.

After moving from the savannah to Nigeria, the ancestors of Kwa speakers began digging wild yams in their new home area. They later switched to farming yams. That change came slowly through selective breeding. If they ate some wild yams that were bitter or harmful, they would keep away from them. If others tasted good, they planted those.

In that way, white and yellow African yams became their staple crop. Those plants provide edible greens and large roots. Within 500 years, farmers in the area were cultivating yams, okra, black-eyed peas, and African groundnuts. Kwa speakers also went from hunting guinea fowls to keeping the birds. As they grew more food, their towns grew larger, too.

Middle Niger Flood Plains

Around 7,000 BCE, the ancestors of Mande speakers left the Sahara as it became drier and more arid. They traveled south to present-day Mali where the Niger River flows through grasslands and scrubs. In the Djenné-Jeno area, they developed iron smelting on a large scale.

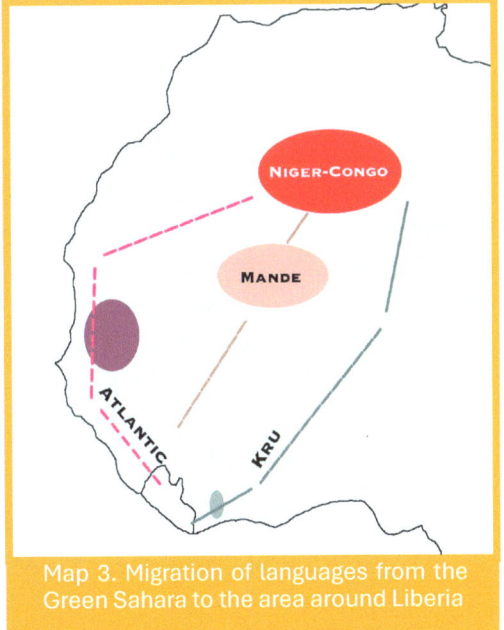

Map 3. Migration of languages from the Green Sahara to the area around Liberia

Iron tools from Djenné-Jeno helped farmers on the Niger River near present-day Bamako. Around 3,500 BCE, they started growing African rice, bottle gourd, watermelon, fonio (a grain used in porridge) and durum wheat (used to make couscous and beer). Within 500 years, they had developed several types of millet, sorghum, and rice. From this area, rice farming spread south along the branches of the Niger River and other coastal river deltas.

The area where Mande speakers settled is near the center of West Africa. For that reason, some Mande speakers became experts in trading. They sold goods back and forth between southern Europe, northern Africa, Arabia, and those West Africans who had moved to live near the forest. Because of long-distance trading, the Mande homeland would become wealthier than many other parts of West Africa.

Southern Mauritania

After leaving the Sahara, the ancestors of the Atlantic language family settled by 6,000 BCE in present-day Mauritania. From there, they spread along the shore of the Atlantic Ocean, down to the forest of present-day Liberia. Linguists call their language by the name of the ocean because most of its speakers live along its coast. Two of the biggest Atlantic-language groups are the Wolof, who excelled at growing swamp rice, and the Fulani, who became expert metal-smelters and herders.

Fulani culture was mainly defined by the keeping, breeding and herding of livestock. Based on the season, herders circulate over a large area each year to graze their livestock. When the heavy rains began falling in the south, they moved into the savanna grasslands of the Sahel. When no rains fell for hundreds of years, people faced hard choices. To avoid famine, some grazed animals at the desert's edge. Others moved east toward the Nile River or south. That shift in climate changed the history of West Africa.

In herding cultures, adults often gave mature youths their own animals to herd. But youths regularly venture away from home to search for new land to graze their cattle, goats or sheep. Driven by the need for new pastures, the Fula communities kept spreading south. By 1,000 BCE, they had occupied the Futa Taro region of Guinea.

Some Atlantic speakers chose a more sedentary lifestyle based on farming rice and millet (also called bulrush). They also discovered many uses for several plants near the forest where they settled. The most important of these plants are the raffia and palm trees. From the fleshy skin of the palm nut, Atlantic speakers derived a nourishing and delicious cooking oil. From the raffia palm tree, they made wine, fiber for rope and roofing for huts, as well as textile for making hats, shoes and decorative mats.

An acrobatic performance. The girls are called "snake babies" because of their ability to contourt their bodies.

Way of the Ancestors

For a very long time, people around the world have sought answers to several deep questions:

- How did life begin?
- What is the purpose of life?
- How do we achieve good?
- How do we attain happiness?
- How can society minimize evil and suffering?
- What happens to humans after we die?

In many places, religion provides the answers. Religion is often treated as separate from everyday life. For answers to these questions, people go to a special place like a church, mosque or temple.

In traditional West Africa, people sought answers in a system they called "the Way of the Ancestors." It provided the framework for society's beliefs and structure. It existed before Niger-Congo split into separate languages 5000 years ago. For that reason, many teachings and practices of that system are found throughout West Africa.

Concept of God

In traditional West African society, God was seen in three ways. One was God the Creator, who was not part of people's everyday life. Another was God the Judge, who supervises people's affairs and intervenes directly. A third was God the hunter, who reaps peoples' essence at the end of life.

According to the Way of the Ancestors, the Creator was all-good, but not all powerful. People originally lived with God, but they were separated at the time of creation. God then filled the world with wonders and powers that are morally neutral.

Controlling Evil

Evil was defined as any action that destroyed the harmony of the community, such as killing, stealing, engaging in adultery, disrespecting elders, lying and doing harm to others. Evil people possessed knowledge of life force and skills which they used for destructive purposes. They manipulated unseen forces to cause mental illness, thefts, business failures, family disputes, ill health, misfortune and death. Even worse, evil people sometimes turned others into wrongdoers with help from charms, spells, and potions to control their bodies and minds. Such behaviors violated all of the sacred norms.

As a result, the world was divided — good from evil, order from disorder, life from death. The Way of the Ancestor sought to preserve good, order and life itself. By teaching the ancestor's norms to children, society preserved the memory of the ancestors and ensured that their rules of behavior were maintained.

The focus of traditional worship and rituals was **life-force**, a vital energy that is present in everyone and everything. We cannot hear, see, touch, smell, or taste life-force, yet it was everywhere. Certain locations had a

For more information, see these:

Bellman, Beryll Larry. *The Language of Secrecy: Symbols and Metaphors in Poro Ritual* (New Brunswick: Rutgers University Press, 1984).

Bourgeois, Arthur P. "Masking in sub-Saharan Africa" (pp. 68-70), in Theodore Celenko, ed., *Egypt in Africa* (Indianapolis: Indiana University Press, 1996).

Harley, George W. *Notes on the Poro in Liberia* (Cambridge, Mass.: Peabody Museum of American Archaeology and Ethnology, Harvard University, 1941).

King, Noel Q. *African Cosmos: An Introduction to Religion in Africa* (Belmont, Calif.: Wadsworth Publishing Co., 1986).

Mitchell, Robert Cameron. *African Primal Religions* (Niles, Ill.: Argus Communications, 1977).

Olupona, Jacob K. ed., *African Spirituality: Forms, Meanings and Expression* (New York: The Crossroad Publishing Co., 2011).

Ray, Benjamin L. *African Religions: Symbol, Ritual, and Community* (Englewoods Cliffs, NJ: Prentice-Hall, 1976).

Sundermeier, Theo. *The Individual and Community in African Traditional Religion* (Piscataway, NJ: Transaction Publishers, 1998).

Zahan, Dominique. *The Religion, Spirituality, and Thought of Traditional Africa* (Chicago: The University of Chicago Press, 1979).

Zuesse, Evan M. *Ritual Cosmos: The Sanctification of Life in African Religions* (Athen, OH: Ohio University Press, 1979).

stronger life-force than others, such as bodies of water, ancient trees and mountains.

Because life-force was unpredictable, the community offered sacrifices and prayers to preserve harmony, good crops, rain, safety and prosperity. Each part of the life-force required its own rituals. As libation to the ancestors, people often offered palm wine, kola or water. To atone for wrongdoing, communities would sacrifice a white chicken, red rooster, sheep or goat.

Although life-force was invisible, it sometimes communicated with people through masquerades and masks. A masquerade wore a special covering at important events or to perform key rituals. The mask was part of their power and hid the person's face and sometimes the head.

While performing the ritual, the wearer of the masquerade and mask became a channel through which the life-force communicated with the community. The wearer became the link between this world and the invisible world of life-force and the ancestors. Only a select few, usually men, were chosen and trained for this honor.

The Dan had a masquerade called **Gbetu** that performs on certain ritual occasions accompanied by music and songs. All adults knew the mask was carved from wood, the body was covered by woven raffia, and its movements were done by a dancer. But, during the *Gbetu's* performance,

Mami Wata

This mythic figure exists in folktales, songs and art across Africa and its Diaspora.

it housed "the force of the forest." To emphasize this transformation, the masquerade usually spoke in a voice that did not sound human.

Other groups had similar masquerades. The **Loma** and **Dan** both had a masquerade on stilts called **Glegben** that was entirely covered in woven fabric. It performed a dance with very intricate hand and feet movements. During the dance, the drummer and the masquerade entered a dialogue with each other. Sometimes the drummer followed the dancer's step and beat. At other times, the dancer followed the rhythms of the drums.

Not all masquerades possessed the same power. The strongest ones appeared at night, sometimes to deliver legal rulings. They were used by old men with influence, especially the head of the founding families. Less powerful masquerades were those created by women and young men for "play" or entertainment. An example of an entertainment masquerade was the **Nafai** of the Vai and Gola which performed during the daytime.

When performing many rituals, policy makers, judges and priests often used masks to symbolize their roles as conduits of life-force. Masks were employed for many purposes, including increased fertility, burial, initiation, law enforcement, adjudication, healing, and divination. Their use was similar to present-day lawyers wearing robes to symbolize their official roles.

While in use, the masquerade became a symbol of a life-force and was considered sacred. When not employed, it was kept in a shrine to protect viewers, especially women and children.

Most masks were made of wood. But a few were ivory, and fewer still were made of brass. Masks and other ritual objects were often decorated with items considered rare and potent. Such items included cowrie shells, feathers, leopard skin, claws of predatory animals, and iron.

Life-Force in Nature

According to the Way of the Ancestors, bodies of water, including rivers and lakes, exuded a powerful life-force which produced good or bad fortune. When

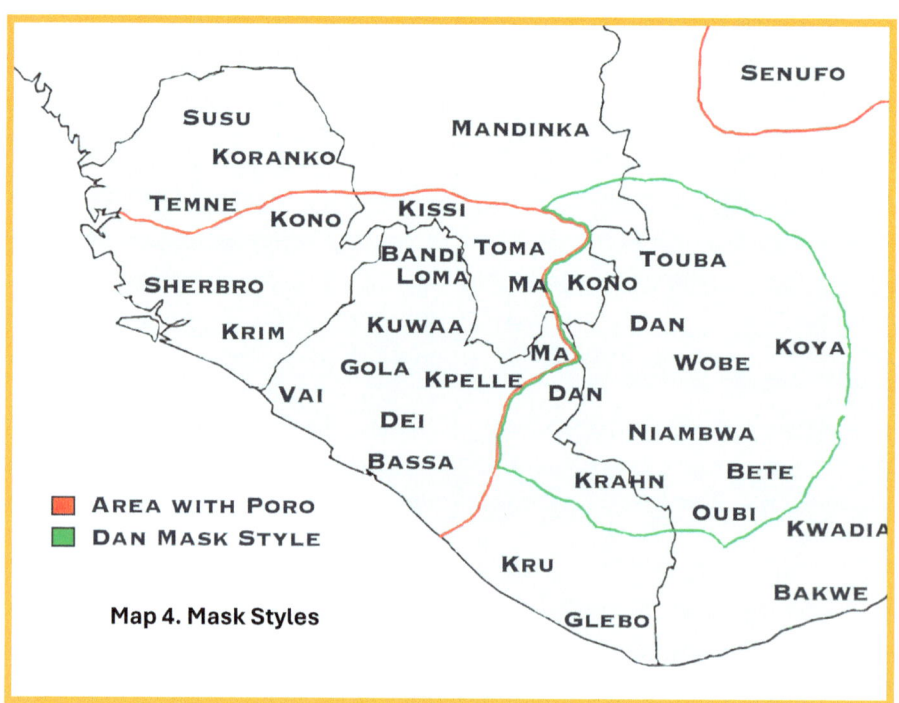

Map 4. Mask Styles

Lessons in morality and logic

In other parts of the world, lessons in morality and logic were written in books. **The Way of the Ancestors** taught similar lessons using verbal arts. To aid recall, those lessons were frequently repeated in group settings. A few examples are given below. Folk tales about **Spider the Trickster** were used to teach young children not to be greedy and selfish. **Dilemna tales** taught reasoning and logic.

How Spider's Waist Became So Thin

Two neighboring villages planned to hold feasts on the same day. Spider, being greedy, wanted to attend both. But he did not know which one would start first. So he tied a rope around his waist. He gave one end to the chief of the first village, and said: "When your feast is about to start, pull this rope."

He tied a second rope about his waist, and he gave the other end to the chief of the second village. Spider also told him to pull the rope when his feast was about to begin.

Spider then waited at a point halfway between the two villages. But the two feasts began at the same time. As a result, one chief pulled against the other chief. As the ropes became tighter and tighter, Spider's waist became smaller and smaller. His waist has been narrow and squeezed in ever since -- all because of **greed**!

Dilemma tale

One man shot through a rock and killed an elephant. Another went through a hole in the rock and brought the elephant back through the hole. When they reached home, they were served the cooked liver of the elephant they had just killed. They called the people and asked them to **judge** which of them excelled the other.

Parables

If a tree does not know how to dance, the wind will teach it.

You cannot be sitting on somebody's head and say the person's hair stinks.

If house don't sell you, street can't buy you.

water forces received respect and offerings, they presented people with gold, gems, business success, and children. People who were taken under water and survived often received gifts like creativity, wisdom and healing skills. If the life force of water was offended, it caused drowning, childlessness, or insanity.

The best-known water creature throughout West Africa was Mami Wata, a beautiful woman with long hair. According to the Way of the Ancestors, she appeared on the beach or the banks of rivers, where she sat combing her hair. If someone persuaded her to give up her comb, she brought them riches to get it back. But, if people were outsmarted by her, they met a tragic end, like drowning. The moral of her story was, "don't be charmed by shallow beauty and false promises."

Power in the Arts

According to the Way of the Ancestors, artists who created ritual art knew how to harness life-force. For example, they did this when they painted or carved images of deceased rulers and other ancestors. The power of those works laid in their ability to connect the past with the present, linking one generation to another. Artists also embedded life-force in ritual objects used at festivals and celebrations. Their success was measured by the power of their creations. If the ritual object led to a successful harvest, it was reused. But if there was a poor harvest, it was thrown away.

To tap the life-force at celebrations, people used music, dance, and colors. Artists revitalized individuals and the community by using certain drumming patterns and dance routines to access the life-force.

Poetry and Proverbs

According to the Way of the Ancestors, words had power. That power was harnessed through poetry, which employed rhythm in speech. In addition, elders transmitted wisdom through condensed and carefully composed speech. A common vehicle was the **proverb**, a piece of advice that was easy to remember because it is short and presented in a clever way. Another popular speech pattern was the **parable**, which is a short story that teaches a hidden lesson.

Visual Symbols

Wisdom was also conveyed using colors and patterns. According to the Way of the Ancestors, four colors had power and symbolic meaning. White symbolized wisdom, tranquility, innocence, and wellbeing. The color white was preferred for sacrificial animals because it symbolized purity. Associated with women, it was used to summon the ancestors and water forces.

Red was reserved for use by priests and middle-aged men. It symbolized blood, vitality, anger, transition and violence. Blue symbolized the life-force of water.

Black suggested raw power, emotion and mystery. It was associated with young men and the life-force of the forest. According to the Way of the Ancestors, a mask or sculpture that was two-toned meant it mediated between the seen and unseen worlds because of its dual nature.

Patterns

Zigzag designs represented water, both in the sky and on land. Sharp angular patterns such as horns and teeth were associated with men, while smooth and naturalistic style were linked to female beauty. Neck rings used on female masks suggested the layering around caterpillars before they turn into butterflies.

Masks and masquerades were an important part of communities in Liberia. All masks and masquerades held deep meanings. Together with dance and song, they portrayed the beliefs and values of the community that produced them. That is why they were featured in important social and ceremonial events. The wearers of the masks occupied a special place in the community, as did the artists who carved the masks. The art of making masks was passed on from father to son, along with the knowledge of the symbolic meanings conveyed by each mask.

Respect for the Ancestors

In the Way of the Ancestors, a person had to earn respect through honorable conduct while living. The status of ancestor was only for those who lived upright lives, acquired wisdom, left descendants, and lived long. Ancestors gained strength and insight after they transitioned to the next phase of life. In the **afterlife,** where there is no violence, their lives continued at a slower pace. For them, death merely brought a change in place.

But not everyone who died became an "ancestor." Death was the end of life for people who lived a dishonorable life. In addition, anyone killed by lightning, drowning, suicide or an unknown disease could not become an ancestor.

A helmet mask of the Sande society. The platted hair was a sign of beauty, the tiny ears a reminder to avoid idle gossip, and the neck rolls symbolized a caterpillar before turning into a butterfly.

Ancestors served as links between their community and God. They helped to protect the society and its **morality**, meaning the values and principles that enable us to distinguish right from wrong. The "ways" of the ancestors were the rules originally set by them. These "ways" became the foundation for law, religion and morality. Because of this, ancestors were involved in punishing anyone who violated society's rules. In short, the living and the dead depended on each other. This meant the living had to live by the rules set by the ancestors to ensure harmony in a community. If not, chaos ensured.

People honored their ancestors in four key ways:

- Symbolically by placing a small Y-shaped ladder with notched steps near an altar to help them climb to God.
- Through libations, using fresh water, millet flour mixed with water, millet beer, or palm wine.
- Offering them the first taste of any prepared food or kola.
- Preserving their memory and passing on their names to descendants.

Fulfilling one's obligations to the ancestors resulted in a happy and prosperous family. Those who failed to honor their ancestors risked bringing bad fortune on themselves and their community.

Shrines and Sacraments

In the Way of the Ancestors, **shrines** and **altars** were placed outdoors. These were usually near natural formations, such as waterfalls, mountains, caves, mysterious rocks and majestic cotton trees.

Many transitions in the life of the community were marked by rituals and sacraments. Rituals were performed before burning the land for planting, after planting, and at harvest.

One sacrament was the rites of passage that transitioned youth from childhood into adulthood. But the most common sacrament was animal sacrifices.

A person wanting to restore health, reveal the future, or increase fertility made a sacrifice of a chicken, goat or cow. Individuals offered sacrifices during other moments of transition, such as birth, adulthood, investiture in political office, or death. Communal sacrifices were required whenever natural disasters occurred, such as flooding or famine. Bigger requests required bigger sacrificial animals.

Workers of Life Energy

In the Way of the Ancestors, rites and rituals were performed by specially selected, initiated and trained individuals. These included priests, prophets, diviners, dancers, wood carvers, blacksmiths and sacred rulers.

African names for months

The Gola name for the first month of the year, **Waaduugbee**, translates to "big dew month." Like the names of months in many local languages, it reflects knowledge of the climate and natural environment.

In contrast, January — the English name for that month — is the name of a pagan Roman god. Yet, it is African cultures that have been dismissed as rooted in "superstitions." And, as a result, it is their knowledge of climate and the environment — as embedded in traditional calendars — that is at risk of being lost.

Diviners

Most villages or towns boasted several diviners. They specialized in reading the future of individual clients. This was done in different ways, including tossing cowrie shells, "cutting" sand, reading the entrails of a sacrificed chicken, casting kola, spinning eggs, or using wisdom to interpret dreams.

Prophets

Unlike the diviners, prophets were concerned with the wellbeing of the community rather than individuals. Prophets could access the unseen world without having to read the kola, sand, or cowrie. With their knowledge and wisdom, they could help a community adjust to social, political, and economic changes. Common examples included migration to a new area, or filtering the impact of new ideas into the community.

Healers

Individuals consulted **healers** on problems of sickness and misfortune. Healers knew the healthful and harmful properties of both plants and animals. They sought to decrease the destructive use of life-force. They did so through protective steps, such as burning appropriate herbs and other items, wearing specific clothes or masks, using chalk or clay to mark the body with sacred symbols, and wearing charms or amulets.

Traditional medicine used a holistic approach to healing, including herbs, counseling, and magic. Healers treated a combination of physical, emotional and other ills which they traced to both invisible and physical causes. In their view, sickness sometimes resulted from invisible sources or an imbalance between the patient and his or her social environment.

Blacksmiths, Weavers and Potters

Of all the specialists capable of controlling life-force, the most respected and powerful were the blacksmiths. Their iron **forges** were sacred. Their **bel-**

lows were used by some groups for swearing oaths. Because few dared to challenge their authority, they often mediated in disputes.

Blacksmiths were the only ones who knew the **alchemy** of fire, land, water, and forest. They could find minerals, create extreme heat, control fire with water, and smelt metals into useful objects. They mastered how to control fire and other dangerous forces needed for working with iron. Because blacksmiths possessed superior knowledge of life-force, they often carried masks, prepared amulets, and presided over **circumcision** at ceremonies marking the transition of youth into adulthood.

According to the Way of the Ancestors, the wives and female relatives of blacksmiths often possessed similar powers. This allowed them to become **weavers** of baskets, bags, fishing nets, fish traps, and various other specialized items. Some of them also became **potters**, making ceramic water jars and cooking pots for household use.

Hunters

Hunters, too, were a highly regarded group because of their primary role as killers of predatory animals and suppliers of meat. Hunters often spent days, weeks and sometimes longer periods in the bush. They survived by learning animal habits and anatomies, as well as the helpful and harmful properties of plants. During their hunts, they lived off the land, eating what they found in the forest. Skillful hunters developed a set of physical skills that made them different from others in the community. Hunters wore unique shirts that made them seem mysterious. Their cotton smocks were **mud-dyed** or stained a rust-brown

Blacksmiths at work

color. Attached to the shirts were horns, claws, strips of leather, and skin-covered **amulets**, which symbolized the life-force of the forest and the animals they had killed.

Artisans and artists

Artisans and artists were respected and sometimes feared because their works embodied powerful yet invisible energy. For that reason, they often conducted specific rituals in their communities. According to the Way of the Ancestors, **leatherworkers** channeled the life-force from the animals whose skins they treated. In a similar way, **wood carvers** absorbed vital energy from the wood they used to make charms and icons. As the number of artisans grew, they formed protective guilds. Those associations guarded their trade secrets and limited competition from outsiders. In the Liberia area, there were guilds formed by blacksmiths, hunters, and **bridge builders**.

Every action that a person did to promote harmony in the community was considered virtuous. Such actions included showing respect for parents and elders, raising children appropriately, providing hospitality, or being honest, trustworthy, and courageous. A good person tried to balance personal and community interests. Through rites and sacraments, traditional authorities tried to channel the powers of the universe to people who used them for good.

Concept of Time

In traditional West African societies, no mechanical clocks or numeral calendars were used to measure time. Instead, time followed the **cycles of nature**. Time was considered **cyclical** and repetitive. In Western culture, time has three dimensions: past, present and future. In traditional African societies, time moved backward from the present to the past, but not forward to the future. Two conditions stood outside of human time: First, the realm of the ancestors, where time operates at a slower speed. Second, the period of creation, which existed beyond time.

In traditional West Africa, time was measured by **days**, **moons** (or months), and **seasons**. For example, an expectant mother would calculate her pregnancy in relation to the number of moons that had passed. The appearance of certain stars in the sky revealed the time for planting crops. The passage of time was also used to measure distance. If asked how far one town was from another, people would say, "it is two days walk," for example.

Time was also measured by **recurring tasks**. Examples included the time for drawing water, market day, and harvest time. The position of the sun in the sky would be used to schedule meetings, such as sunrise, noon, or sunset.

Finally, time was measured by a calendar of **sacred rituals**. The time to celebrate each ritual was determined by natural events like the full moon or tasks, such as harvest time.

Basket of salt; kola plant and seeds; malagueta plant and spices.

Salt, Kola & Malagueta, 410 - 1085 CE

The first groups to migrate from the Sahel to present-day Liberia were the Atlantic and Kru speakers. Those ancestors of Liberians bravely faced many problems as they settled in the forest region. Despite the hardships they encountered, they established lasting **social structures** that have survived to this day.

The Atlantic speakers began their journey in Mauritania around 6,000 BCE. They traveled down the coast through Senegal and The Gambia before entering Guinea, Sierra Leone and Liberia. As there are no references to water travel in their origin stories, it seems likely that they came by land rather than by river or sea.

When they arrived, the Liberian forest region was filled with wildlife, including pygmy hippopotami, forest elephants, and water buffalos. According to oral histories, the few people living in the area were unusual. Both Kru and Atlantic groups say their ancestors met very short people in the territory now called Liberia. According to the Gola, the so-called "Pygmies" lived in caves and the hollows of large trees; their diet consisted of fruit and roots.

These claims seem possible for two reasons: First, "**Pygmies**" live in Africa's other major forest belt in the **Congo**. Second, Liberia is home to many pygmy animal species, including hippopotamus and antelope. If there were Pygmies, their numbers soon dwindled. They probably died out or were absorbed by the incoming groups.

Oral traditions from western Liberia say the **Gola** were the first Atlantic group to settle in the area. According to Gola oral tradition, they were initially a small, isolated group living in a homeland called **Mana** in the northwestern mountains of Liberia.

The **Kissi**, another Atlantic-language group, also settled in the Liberia area around this time. The Kissi and **Gola** were only 80 miles apart, but their languages were vastly different. Such sharp differences suggest their languages separated a long time ago.

In a shelter cut into a rock between Bolahun and Kolahun near the Kaihar River, archaeologists have found stone tools, the base of a large pot, charcoal, and burned palm oil. Those findings, plus oral tradition and linguistic evidence, suggest some ancestors of Atlantic speakers were in the interior of western Liberia by 450 CE. Similar evidence from the **Po River** area suggest that Kru-speakers were living along the coast of western Liberia by 900 CE. They were likely the ancestors of the **Dei**.

Kru-speakers migrated from the area of Burkina Faso down the **Kamoé River** in Côte d'Ivoire to the edge of the forest. They then turned west and into the **Nzo Valley**. At this time, large numbers of **Gur** and **Kwa-speaking** groups were already living in those places. Some Kru-speakers then continued their migration west toward **Mount Gedeh**.

The first signs of people living in eastern Liberia date from 410 to 1085

For more information, see these:

Brooks, George E. *Kola Trade and State Building: Upper Guinea Coast and Senegambia, 15th and 17th Centuries* (Boston, MA: Boston University, African Studies Center, 1980).

Bureau of Folkways, *The Tribes of the Western Province and the Denwoin People* (Monrovia: Bureau of Folkways, Interior Department, 1955).

Hair, P. E. H. "Ethnolinguistic of the Upper Guinea coast before 1700," *African Languages Review* VI: 32-70.

Horton, Robin. "Stateless societies in the history of West Africa" (pp. 78-119), in J. F. Ade Ajayi and Michael Crowder, *History of West Africa*, Vol. I (New York: Columbia University Press, 1972).

Massing, Andreas W. "A Segmentary Society Between Colonial Frontiers: The Kissi of Liberia, Sierra Leone and Guinea, 1892-1913," *Liberian Studies Journal*, IX, 1 (1980-1981).

Person, Yves. "Les Kissi et leurs statuettes de pierre dans le cadre de l'histoire ouest-africaine," *Bulletin de l'Institute francais d'Afrique noire*, Série B, t, XXIII, no. 1-2, (1961), Annexes.

Person, Yves. "Des Kru en Haute-Volta," *Bulletin de l'Institute francais d'Afrique noire*, Série B, t. 28 (1967): 485-492.

Schwab, George. *Tribes of the Liberian Hinterland*, Peabody Museum Papers, No. 31 (Cambridge, Mass.: Harvard University Press, 1947).

Smith, Robert. "The canoe in West African history," *Journal of African History*, Vol. II, No. 4 (1970): 515-533.

Van Harten, A. M. "Melegueta pepper," *Economic History* 24 (1970): 208-217.

Wilson, W. A. A. "Atlantic" (pp. 81-104), in John Bender Samuel (ed.), *The Niger-Congo Languages* (Lanham, MD: University Press of American, 1989).

CE. In Sanniquelli, archaeologists found small pieces of broken pots, charcoal, stone tools, **shards** of clay pots, and oil-palm. It is likely that the Kru-speaking groups left the artifacts discovered at **Sanniquelli**, **Grand Gedeh** and **Po River**.

Clans, Family and Kinship

From earliest time, the basic building blocks of Niger-Congo societies were clans, families and kinship. A **clan** consisted of all who descended from a common ancestor. In other words, members of a clan were those born from a single founding ancestor through the male line. Most clans lived in a village of 100-200 residents or in their own section of a town.

It seems Niger-Congo societies were originally matrilineal. That meant property and title were inherited from the mother's family or the brother of one's mother. Men who were seeking a wife worked for their in-laws before marriage and joined the wife's clan after marriage. After 1063 CE, men usually held political authority in the clan and in society more broadly.

Layout of Villages

Human spaces were often arranged according to **patterns in nature**. Because women give birth, they are associated with the east, the direction from which the sun rises or is "born." In contrast, men are linked to the west, the direction of the sun's death (sunset). In keeping with this code, villages were laid out so female Sande "gardens" were in the east and male Poro groves in the west.

Family Units

The basic family unit began with a marriage; it ended either with the death of one spouse or divorce. Each **nuclear family** was composed of a husband, his wife and their children. In addition, some families in West Africa were **polygamous**; they were composed of a man, his several wives, and their children. But most men could not afford to support multiple wives. For that reason, mainly wealthy men had polygamous families.

Besides nuclear and polygamous families, West Africans maintained **extended families**. These units had relatives from several generations. It was common for such households to include other relatives of the father, such as unmarried sisters, aged parents, and the children of the father's clan sent to be raised by him. In such cases, his wife or wives took on all the heavy social roles demanded of a mother or daughter. Families rarely showed a difference how they treated so-called "blood" relatives and non-biological kin.

Residents and Strangers

Kinship rules governed the relations between husband and wife, between parents and children, and between siblings. It was the elders of the family who decided who could marry eligible women. They also provided the resources young relatives needed to get married. In exchange, junior family members and dependents owed elders deference, respect, and labor.

Each village was governed by a **hierarchical system** based on kinship. The head of the clan governed the production of food and growth of the population. He **judged** internal disputes, approved new residents, and divided farmland controlled by the clan, presided over ceremonies, and represented the clan in dealings with other groups.

While villages often absorbed outsiders, "strangers" gained access to resources over time by respecting the rules of the community. Newcomers to a village earned a place in the community by giving gifts or providing labor. Among the Dan, a typical present was a onetime gift to the clan ruler of a gown made from homespun cotton. Among the Kpelle, "strangers" were expected to give crops or meat annually. It often took many years before newcomers were considered full members of the community.

Elders and Youth

Elders were usually men known for their wisdom, good behavior, and long-standing ties to the community. They were responsible to preserve the community and to keep it working properly. They selected the leader of the clan and judged disputes.

Although men usually exercised public leadership, many women held parallel, complementary or even superior positions, especially after child-bearing age. Their status was conferred based on the belief that they had sacred power and could act as **conduits** for God, the ancestors and the **life-force**.

While young women assisted their mothers with household and some farming chores, young men helped with planting, farming, hunting, and fishing, as well as gathering palm wine, palm nuts, and kola nuts.

Tensions within the Clan

The kinship system was not free from internal conflicts. The **competition** over marriageable women sometimes caused tensions between elders and young men. In a similar way, junior wives quarreled with senior wives over tasks. Junior brothers also competed fiercely with senior brothers for their fathers' property. When quarrels boiled over, young men often left the village, cleared new land, and branched off. They became the founding members of their village, with their leader as the new clan head.

Among Atlantic and Mande groups, houses were usually round, with roofs made of woven palm matting. In southeastern Liberia, buildings among Kru-speakers were usually rectangular with ridged roofs.

Challenges of the Forest

For the ancestors of the Gola, Kissi, Dei and Klao, living in the savannah was hard. But settling in the forest belt was far more difficult. The Liberian forests

Power & Influence in Village Communities

Our ancestors valued knowledge. Sometimes it came from age. Other men with high standing were specialists such as blacksmiths.

2 Male Elders & Specialists

1 Clan Leader

An elder choosen on the basis of wisdom, integrity, strength or other leadership qualities.

3 Female Elders & Specialists

Midwives, herbalists, Sande Society leader, and representative of the family that settled the land first.

4 Men

Men usually gained access to a community through their ancestors. If they were strangers, they worked to earned a place. In farming areas, men cut trees, burned fields and built huts. In other places, they herded animals or traveled far to buy and sell things.

5 Women

If men held power in a society, a woman's connection was often through her father or husband. Women's work included gardening, caring for children, fetching water and local trading.

6 Children

Children helped with chores. A boy usually learned his father's job.

teemed with dangerous wildlife, such as leopards, bush cows, and elephants. The fear that those ancestors first felt when they encountered the forest is enshrined in the folktales they left behind. In the founding tales of many groups, the heroes had to deal with their fear of predatory animals as they hunted for meat. Among the scariest characters in local folktales are forest spirits, known as *lausing* in **Kpelle**.

The forest was a source of other dangers. The **tsetse fly** infested both people and cows with African sleeping sickness. Then there were the always-present mosquitos that carry many deadly diseases such as malaria, encephalitis, dengue and yellow fevers.

Physically, the forest was hard to travel through. People had to cut down trees in order to build towns and to till soil for planting crops. Much of the soil is **laterite**. Because it is rich in iron, it turns red when exposed to rain for a while. Laterite forms reddish pebbles that can become 30-feet thick, making it very difficult to farm.

The climate presents another challenge to farming and other human activities. Along the coast, the rains fall from March to July and then from September to mid-November. During the rainy season, rains fall almost unceasingly day and night. Areas with heavy rains have many thriving plants, while areas that have less rain have fewer plants. But the heavy rainfall can bring floods that devastate people, their homes, the soil, and plants.

> **Atlantic languages at risk**
>
> Atlantic is a family of 65 languages. They are very diverse, which makes it difficult to uncover patterns among them.
>
> At least 13 Atlantic languages have less than 10,000 speakers. Some of these languages, like Gola (Liberia) and Kissi (Sierra Leone, Liberia and Guinea), are surrounded by Mande speakers. As a result, they are being replaced by the languages of their neighbors.
>
> Atlantic speakers have generally lived in hamlets, not large compact towns. For that reason, smaller languages in this family are at risk of becoming extinct.

November is the beginning of the dry season. The sun dries the ground and slowly bakes the soil. The Gola call this month **Bobo**, or "swamp hard." As the soil dries, plants begin to wilt and die from the lack of moisture. In addition, from the end of November until March, the **Harmattan**, a hot dry wind, blows from the Sahara. Clouds of fine sand and dust in the air make it difficult to breathe. They cover everything in a thin film of red dust.

People new to living in the forest faced a constant struggle to provide the necessities of life, such as tools, food, shelter, and clothing. Many Liberian folktales tell of frequent "**hungry times**" and migrations because of famine. Others tell of tensions and even conflicts between communities. Despite hardships, people moved to the forest area to create new towns and farms. They established traditions that ensured harmony and the continuity of life.

Trade and Farming

The ancestors of Gola, Kissi, Dei, and Klao Liberians brought skills with them that became the basis for agriculture and trade in the area. Though they splintered from the larger Atlantic and Kru speaking groups, these migrants in the forests did not live in isolation but remained tied to other groups through trade.

Locally made iron tools assisted in farming. Local **commodities** influenced the opening and closing of trade routes, the migration of language groups, and even the rise and fall of empires in the Sahel. Four products of the forest area dramatically affected the history of West Africa: kola seeds, malagueta spice, salt, and rice.

Salt is essential to human survival because the body will not function properly without it. People living in the coastal area of present-day Liberia had unlimited access to salt from the sea. But people living away from the coast faced

Map 5. Kru languages in Burkina Faso, Côte d'Ivoire and Liberia

a chronic shortage, including those along the Niger River. This made salt a good item for trade between the coast and the inland areas.

Many oral traditions suggest the Dei were the first to produce salt from sea water. Archaeologists have found elaborate pottery on the Atlantic coast just west of the Po River dating from 900 to 1085 CE. These pots were apparently used to distill salt water.

> ### Kru languages & cultures
>
> Kru is a family of 41 languages spoken mainly in Liberia and Côte d'Ivoire. These languages are not closely related to neighboring coastal Kwa languages as once thought.
>
> They are more related to Aizi (an isolated language in Côte d'Ivoire) and Siamon (spoken in the Orodara region of Burkina Faso).
>
> Approxiatey eight Kru languages have less than 10,000 speakers, including Kuwaa and Dei in Liberia, placing them in danger.
>
>
>
> **Kru iron ring,
> which also served as money**

Pottery and Long-Distance Salt Trade

An oral legend gives us clues about the origin of the Dei. It says the group's first ancestors were a local woman (probably women) and a maritime man (probably men) who arrived from the north along the St. Paul River. The story says the man presented a metal ring and a coin to the woman. In addition, he paid his dowry with a finely decorated drum that was made from multiple metals. These references to metals suggest the male ancestors of the Dei brought knowledge of metalworking when they migrated.

Dei oral tradition says that **Kambai Bli** (a town along the road to Bomi Hills) is their oldest town. It was the site of a large clay pit for producing pottery products that attracted buyers from afar. For that reason, it was economically important.

The primary source of Dei wealth was salt boiling. Their ancestors who made salt lived along the beach from the mouth of the St Paul River to Cape Mount. Their towns included **Duojena**, **Dugbei**, **Gakpoja**, and **Mbaanwoin**.

The Dei say their ancestors founded **Bopolu** as a trade town where they exchanged salt for products from the north. Originally called **Taabli** (Taa's town), it became a regular stop for trade caravans from elsewhere in West Africa.

Bopolu was just one of many towns established by the people in the forest and woodlands for trading. Those sites were located miles away from their homes, workshops and raw materials. They provided a place to meet with visiting traders without giving outsiders access to the knowledge of their resources.

Origin of the Kola Trade

As early as 1200 CE, kola was available in European markets. Oral traditions as well as studies of African languages and early trade routes all suggest that the ancestors of the Gola first developed a northward trade in kola nuts. Among the **Temme** (former neighbors of the Gola) the word for Kola is **kola** or **tola**, and kola trees are known as **nola** or **yola.**

Kola grows in areas north of Sierra Leone, Guinea and Liberia. It is found as far east as the Congo River. But those trees usually produce nuts that are eaten locally because they are too small to trade. The land first settled by the Gola produced the most desirable kola.

The large kola tree bears a pod of about six seeds that fall to the ground when ripe. The most widely sold varieties of kola contain caffeine, which made kola a popular ingredient in soft drinks around the world.

The use of kola is embedded in cultures throughout West Africa. People use it in divination ceremonies; they give it to guests as a sign of hospitality; they present it to strangers to show a "clean heart;" and they offer it to the ancestors out of respect.

Export of Malagueta Spice

Malagueta spice was used to season food. It originally grew only in swampy areas between River Cess and Cape Palmas. By 1214 CE, malagueta was on sale in Italy and Spain, where people called it "Grain of Paradise," "Guinea Grain," and "Alligator Pepper." Doctors in several European countries prescribed it to their patients as a cure for various ailments.

The malagueta bush produces a solid yellowish green stems and pink flowers shaped like trumpets. Its berries are small, narrow, pungent, and contain many small brown seeds.

The spice was probably traded north by the **Kru**-speaking people who lived between River Cess and Cape Palmas. From the Sahel, camel caravans took it across the Sahara to the harbor of **Mud'barca** near **Tripoli** in North Africa and across the Mediterranean Sea to **Italy**. It also found its way into Spain, which suggests the use of another trade route.

Navigating Winds and Currents

Kru-speakers in the southeastern region of present-day Liberia excelled in carving, iron-smelting, and growing malagueta spice. Those living in interior towns carved canoes out of a single tree trunk. They then sold them to people living along the coast. Canoes plied the Atlantic Ocean, as well as most of the lagoons and navigable rivers throughout the region. Ancestors of the Kru-speaking groups probably first developed their knowledge of water travel while living in the Sahel. They adapted their skills for use along the Atlantic coast.

According to Klao oral tradition, their ancestors came from the north and settled at **Pisiyo Sigli**. From there they moved south to the coast where they set up the towns of **Kankiya**, **Matiye** on the Nonbwa River and **Tuglo** and **Siglipo**. The town of Kankiya was destroyed by the waters of the Nonbwa River, and *Siglipo* was renamed Grand Cess. Later Klao ancestors established other towns on the coast such as **Pakyo**, **Papukio** and **Tubwegh**.

Klao oral traditions state that the towns of Little Kroo, Sestra Kroo, Kroo-Bar, Nana-Kroo and King Willis Town were founded by seafarers from present-day Ghana. This seems supported by the shared value of the **Aggrey** or **Popo** beads- small blue pipe beads imported from the Gold Coast. The Klao and Fanti in what is now known as Ghana traveled by canoe to trade with each other.

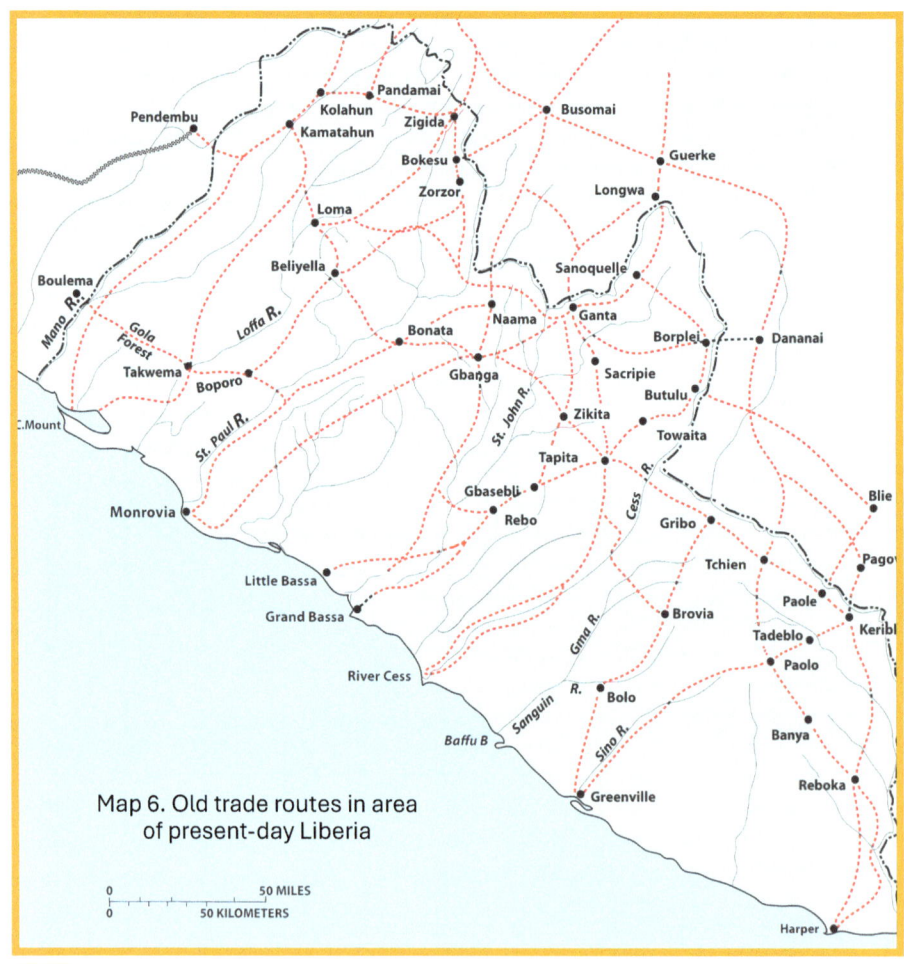

Map 6. Old trade routes in area of present-day Liberia

Because large game and livestock were rare near the Atlantic Ocean, coastal communities depended on fish and other seafood. For them, fishing became as important as hunting was to those living in the forest area. Using paddles to propel each canoe, seafarers fished, transported passengers, and traded dried fish, among other goods.

Coastal residents developed a sophisticated understanding of seasonal ocean currents, wind patterns, and the habits of various sea creatures. Coastal people built their towns near freshwater sources, such as creeks or rivers. Bays along the coast provided natural harbors and reefs, which were habitats for fish. Lagoons proved ideal sites for towns because they provided drinking water.

Rice Farming

The **rice belt** of West Africa today overlaps the area inhabited by the Atlantic speakers. For that reason, it seems likely the ancestors of Kissi and Gola brought rice farming with them to the Liberia area. In particular, the Kissi were called the "**rice people**" because they grew more of it than their neighbors. In the area now called Liberia, people farmed rice mainly near the coast and in the savannah west of the St. John River. In those areas, it was possible to reap three harvests of swamp rice every year.

Iron working was a central feature of Kissi culture. Pontan sculptures, like the one on the left, were carved from stones with iron tools. Kissi blacksmiths also made twisted iron bars that circulated as money.

Rice farming in the forest belt was intensive work. It required many strong workers to clear the fields. Harvesting demanded the participation of several families, since it was a race against the birds and wild animals.

The ancestors of Liberians often divided the tasks of rice farming according to sex and age. Adult men cleared the fields, while boys chased away pests with slingshots, rocks, and musical instruments. Women planted, weeded, harvested, hulled, and, of course, cooked the rice.

Iron Working

Before 100 BCE, settlements in the forest belt were small clearings made with stone tools and controlled burning. Those villages usually straddled a single road or bank of a river. After iron tools became available to fell trees, people created larger farming communities. In traditional villages, the family whose ancestors first farmed the land held it in sacred trust. The community elders decided who received land for farming and how much.

Several clues point to the ancestors of the Kissi as engaged in **iron working**. For many centuries, they lived near iron deposits and used smelted iron as money. In addition, oral traditions credit ancestors of the Kissi as the creators of ancient stone statues that depict iron axes and spears. Those sculptures are found buried in scattered fields throughout the border region of Liberia, Sierra Leone and Guinea.

Called **pomtan** by the Kissi, the stone statues are 3 to 6 inches tall and made from hard stones. For that reason, they were probably carved by blacksmiths who produced iron tools and wood carvings. As blacksmiths traveled from town to town selling their wares, they likely helped to spread the statues in many areas.

People of the Poro and Sande Societies

According to many oral histories in western Liberia, the Gola started two organizations to preserve the Way of the Ancestors. One was called the **Poro**, which united men, while the **Sande** did the same for women. The two associations later spread to the Kissi, Bandi, Kuwaa, Loma, Bassa, Kpelle and some Dan groups. Many other groups in the West African forest belt eventually adopted the two associations.

The Poro and Sande were led by powerful elders commonly known as Zoes and Mazos. Their decisions applied to everyone in the community. Anyone who disobeyed a decision became an outcast. The identities of Poro and Sande leaders were hidden behind masks when announcing important verdicts and decisions. The masks indicated that the leaders' actions and decisions reflected the will of the collective, not of individuals.

The Poro and Sande served several important community functions. First, they initiated youth into adult life. Their rites of passage varied in length from several months to years. During the rites, a child's attachments to the nuclear family were supplemented by ties to peers and elders within the community. Second, they strengthened trade and intermarriage between villages. By collaborating across ethnic lines, they were better able to promote local trade and defend traditions. Third and most importantly, they preserved the Way of the Ancestors, meaning, those customs and beliefs forged thousands of years before West Africans were scattered by the drying of the Sahara.

West African **cotton cloth** were among popular exports to Europe.

Trade and Migrations, 700-1230 CE

According to linguists, the Mande language originated in the southern Sahara. But the drying of the Sahara forced Mande-speakers south to the Sahel around 300 BCE in search of water and fertile land. Along the Niger River, they established farming and trading communities. Their extensive trade networks reached throughout West Africa, as well as far-flung markets in Europe and Asia. With profits from long-distance trade, Mande-speakers forged magnificent empires. But trade brought new ideas that challenged the Way of the Ancestors and other traditions.

Between 100 and 1500 CE, the Mande language separated into northern, southwestern, and southeastern branches. A smaller branch, called Mandekan, developed around the gold fields of Bambuk and Bouré.

The northern Mande speakers further split into four major groups based on religion and location. Those who held on to the Way of the Ancestors were called **Soso** in Senegambia, Guinea and Sierra Leone. They were known as **Soninké** in Upper Niger, Upper Guinea and southern Senegambia. In the east, they use the name **Bambara**.

Mande speakers who converted to Islam spoke a language called **Malinké**. Among them were traders called the **Dyula** clan, who spread throughout West Africa. As early as 1200 CE, they established trading posts in places currently known as the Republic of Guinea, Cape Mount, Côte d'Ivoire, and Ghana. Their long-distance trading brought great wealth to their homeland along the Niger.

Trade Networks

From 700 CE, trading slowly transformed the Sahel. Those changes also influenced life in the forests of West Africa. By 1200 CE, societies throughout West African were selling many goods to distant markets. Trade networks crisscrossed West Africa, running north to south and east to west. Merchants carried goods across the forests, savanna, Sahel, and Sahara. They moved goods into and out of Africa.

Within West Africa, people exchanged goods they produced for things they wanted from other communities. Locally traded items included sorghum, gold, salt, strips of cloth, iron bars, copper, silver, kola and, later, enslaved Africans. A key trade item was salt. Some came from the **Taoudenni** rock-salt mines of Mali, while coastal towns in present-day Liberia supplied sea salt. Without the salt trade, people living in areas that did not produce salt would die.

Moving goods from place-to-place required well-established networks. Merchants created fixed places where they could sell imported goods to farmers, miners and salt makers. Both buyers and sellers needed goods to be in the markets on time. That was possible only if trade networks were reliable.

In present-day Liberia, one such network ran from the mouth of the St.

For more information, see these:

Brooks, George E. **Western Africa to c. 1860 A. D.** (Bloomington: African Studies Program, Indiana University, 1985).

Coquery-Vidrovitch, Catherine & Paul E. Lovejoy (eds.), **The Workers of African Trade** (Beverly Hills: Sage, 1985).

Devisse, J. "Trade and trade routes in West Africa" (pp. 190-214) in I. Hrbek, ed., **General History of Africa**, Vol. III. Berkeley: University of California Press, 1992).

Jones, Adam. "Who are the Vai?" **Journal of African History** 22 (1981): 159-178.

Levtzion, Nehemia. "The early states of the Western Sudan to 1500" (pp. 120-157), in J. F. A. Ajayi and M. Crowder, **History of West Africa**, Vol. I (New York: Columbia University Press, 1972).

Massing, Andreas W. "The Wangara, an old Soninke diaspora in West Africa?" **Cahiers d'etudes africains**, 158, XL-2 (2000): 218-308.

Moseley, Katherine P. "Caravel and caravan: West Africa and the World-Economies ca. 900-1900 AD," **Review**, Vol. 15, No. 3 (Summer 1992): 523-555.

Perinbam, B. Marie. "Social relations in the trans-Saharan and Western Sudanese trade: An overview," **Comparative Studies in Society and History**, 15, 4 (Sep. 1973): 416-436.

Rashid, Ismail. "Class, caste & social inequality in West African history" (pp. 118-140), in E. K. Akeyampong (ed.), **Themes in West Africa's History** (London: James Currey, 2006).

Tamari, Tal. "The development of caste systems in West Africa," **Journal of African History** 32 (2).

Vydrine, Valentin. "Who Speaks 'Mandekan'?: A note on current use of Manding and Mande ethnonyms and linguonyms," **MANSA Newsletter**, 29 Winter 1995-96): 6-9.

Paul River through **Bopolu**, to **Musadu** in the Republic of Guinea, and then up to the Niger River. Merchants carried malagueta spice and kola nuts to markets as far as Europe. Another minor route connected the Atlantic coastal area near Freetown, Sierra Leone, to the **Taghaza Trail** in the northern section of present-day Mali.

The various connected routes allowed goods to reach all parts of West Africa. Big towns along the routes held key marketplaces. They also gave merchants and their animals opportunities to eat, drink, and rest.

Donkeys and Waterways

To move goods easily and quickly, traders used transportation suited to the different terrains of West Africa. In the forest, transportation was difficult. Pack animals could not survive because of diseases spread by the tsetse fly. Having no animals suitable for carrying goods, merchants relied on human porters. It was common to see groups of several hundred porters and merchants taking their products to the Sahel.

In the Savanna, donkey caravans carried goods from one major town to the next. Donkeys are like cousins of horses, but they are slower. Donkey caravans included up to hundreds or even several thousand animals.

Between 700 CE and 1100 CE, West Africa entered a wet period. Rivers that were once shallow became deep enough to allow boats to carry goods. Lakes increased in size and became home to many more fish. The change in climate also affected the land. The forest expanded north by about 310 miles, moving

Caravan of porters crossing a river

into the woodland savannah. The Sahel became savannah, and the Sahara shrank making it easier to transport goods across the smaller area of desert lands. People moved to areas that were previously dry.

In this period, swollen rivers became routes for moving goods to markets across West Africa. They also supplied fish for people to eat, water for them to drink, and irrigation for farming.

Towns sprang up along the banks of major waterways. Navigable rivers such as Senegal, Niger, Volta and Benue all flowed down to the Atlantic Ocean. Seafarers along the Atlantic coast ferried goods to the mouths of the rivers. From small towns along the rivers, boats carried goods to the major river ports of Djenne, Gao, and Timbuktu. From those places, traders loaded goods onto camels and took them to destinations beyond the desert.

Crossing the Sahara

The **Assyrians** probably first brought camels to North Africa around 600 CE, when they invaded Egypt. Within 300 years, the camels had multiplied, and some were taken west into the Sahara. Because of them, the desert was no longer a barrier. By 100 BCE, they had replaced the oxen and horses for travel in the desert.

Camels were ideal for crossing the Sahara. First, they can withstand the dry conditions and extreme temperatures in the desert, where temperatures reach as high as 135.8 degrees

Donkeys in the Sahel

Fahrenheit in the day and below 32 degrees Fahrenheit at night. Second, they only need to drink water every eight to ten days. Third, the pads on the bottom of their feet spread out when they walk, which prevents them from sinking into the sand. No other pack animal could survive such harsh conditions.

Camels also are well-suited for long-distance trading. For example, they can carry up to 330 pounds in weight, which is twice as much as oxen. In addition, they travel about 8 to 10 miles per hour. That makes them faster than other pack animals. Finally, they can walk for roughly 18 hours at a time before they need to rest.

"Ships of the Desert"

Minor routes within West Africa were connected to major ones be-

Camel caravan in the Sahara

yond the region. Trade routes in the west and the east ran along the fringes of the Sahara. The **Taghaza Trail** in the west connected Senegal to Morocco. It ran northwards through southern Mauritania, Sijilmasa in Morocco, and on to the oasis town of Aoudaghost near Fez in Morocco. In the east, a track connected Lake Chad to Jabal Nafusa in Libya.

Another route ran from east to west. It went from Walata across the Sahara to Agadez and Bilma before turning north to **Cairo** in Egypt. Several northern routes connected trade cities like Timbuktu, **Jenne** and **Gao** in the Sahel to cities like Ghadames and the Mediterranean ports in present-day Algeria, Morocco, Libya, and Tunisia.

Camel caravans crossed the desert following fixed routes. They went from one **oasis** (or source of water) to another, until they reached their destination. Merchants and their animals could die from a lack of water if they veered away from those routes.

Caravans would set out around dawn, when the desert was still cool. Before noon, they would stop at an oasis to avoid traveling when the desert was extremely hot. At each stop, merchants secured their camels and unpacked their loads. If there were no trees for shade, merchants rested under a stretched-out cloth until the heat of the day passed. Their journey resumed at sunset and continued until midnight, using the stars as their guide.

On the backs of camels, traders in the Sahel sent their goods north across the desert to places in North Africa, the Middle East and Europe in exchange for exotic goods. Camel caravans consisted of 2,000 to 20,000 animals. For that reason, the Sahara was often called "the great sand sea" and camels the "ships of the desert."

Foreign goods imported into Africa flowed through international trade networks. By 1300 CE, for example, cowry shells from the Indian Ocean in the east became part of local cultures. Those shells served as decoration, currency, and tools for fortunetelling. Arabs brought the cowries to East Africa by **dhows**, before transporting them along the east-west land route to West Africa. Beginning 300 years later, traders also imported bananas, plantains, chickens, copper, and ceramics to West Africa along the same routes.

From the Mediterranean region and Europe, merchants brought beads, ceramics, glass, oil lamps, saffron, dates, and wheat flour to West Africa. Also imported were luxury items like brass vessels, glassware, tailored clothes, beads, mirrors, perfumes and paper.

From time to time, small groups of Mande speakers would move from the Sahel to the forest belt. The first wave consisted mainly of traders, farmers, and weavers wanting better opportunities. Some were seeking to avoid conversion to Islam. Their migrations into the forests were slow, occurring over many years. They were searching for the best areas for farming, available mineral resources and other commodities to trade. They would settle in an area for several years before deciding to stay or move to another area.

From Farming to Trading

The Mande-speaking communities in the Sahel were originally organized according to the kinship system, like the Gola, Kissi, Dei, Klao, and other forest groups. That system assigned political and sacred power to elders from the family that first claimed the land.

Using wealth from trading, people living in the Sahel created several powerful states, known as empires. Empires combine many cultures, ethnic groups, or nations under the control of one supreme ruler. What began as ethnic units of several thousand people expanded to empires with millions of subjects.

From around 1230 CE to 1450 CE, three empires In West Africa dominated the region. They were **Ghana** (300-1077 CE), **Kaniaga** (1180-1213) and **Mali** (1235-1450). Those states were envied by merchants and rulers in Europe, the Middle East, and elsewhere. Some empires had fixed boundaries. In other cases, their borders fluctuated depending on allegiances and available resources.

The main source of wealth shifted from farming to trading. That shift challenged the kinship system. Merchants had little need to farm because they could buy the food and other necessities of life.

West African Exports to Europe

In 632 CE, Arabs pushed across North Africa and into Spain. Around 1000 CE, the religion of Islam entered West Africa. It was brought by Berber Muslim traders from North Africa who served as hosts to other Muslims traders. They later joined with the converted Mandinka to forge a link to a Muslim trading chain that stretched as far east as China. Although the rulers of West African empires initially held onto the Way of the Ancestors, they used Muslim scholars to help administer their governments. Some of those scholars considered local traditions to be unacceptable. The rulers also gave Muslim merchants, scholars and scribes permission to live in a separate city with their own mosques and schools.

Arabs expanded demand for African exported goods like kola, malagueta, and cotton cloth to markets in northern Africa and Europe. Even more important exports were gold and ivory.

As early as 1100 CE, West African cotton cloth was being exported to Europe. It was woven on narrow looms, mainly by men. In Arabic, West African cotton cloth was known as *barrakan*. In Europe, it was called *barra cana*, *bucaranum* or *boqueranus*. Those words were derived from *barinkan*, the Mande word for "garment."

Of all the items exported from West Africa, gold was the most sought after. After 1200 CE, the gold coins of Europe were minted mainly from West African ore.

The merchants who first brought gold nuggets from the Sahel to Europe and the Muslim world also brought rumors of vast goldmines in the region. But West African rulers kept the location of the gold mines a closely guarded secret. They did this by conducting all business transactions with foreign

Gold and Ivory were two major exports to Europe. Mali supplied two-thirds of the gold used by Mediterranean countries to make coins and jewelry. Ivory was used to to make plaques and piano keys.

traders far from the gold mines. Over time, trading changed the fundamental social structure of Sahelian society. As this long-distance trade flourished across West Africa, it led to endless rivalries and hostilities between factions seeking to control the flow of goods. To protect the empire and its trade routes, rulers created armies composed of foot soldiers and troops on horses. The new male warrior class also challenged the social structure.

Another challenge came from the newly introduced religion of Islam brought to West Africa by Arab merchants. The major trade routes in the region served as conduits for the new religion. Some routes connected West Africa to the Middle East. Other routes linked the Sahel with Islamic North Africa.

By 1351 CE, an earlier matrilineal structure was pushed aside by a patrilineal system. This new structure emerged because of pressure from male warriors, as well as the influence of Arab culture, which was patrilineal. However, women continued to hold political office, engage in full-time trade, and possess wealth independent of their husbands. This was very different from many parts of Europe and the Middle East where men exercised far more control over women.

From Clans to Castes

At the same time, the old social structure of farming was displaced by a new hierarchical caste system tied to occupation. At the top of the caste system were the traders followed by the traditional farmers, fishermen, warriors and animal breeders. At the bottom was the slave caste made up of people whose ancestors were enslaved due to wars between ethnic groups. They were non-Malinke people. Above the castes was the political ruler.

In this new order, traders replaced the elders and religious men as the leaders of the communities. Merchants had increased their power through arranged alliances with other traders throughout West Africa. These alliances were built by sending their sons to apprentice with other traders and by arranging for the children of widely scattered traders to marry each other. Through this system, merchants expanded their influence and trading areas.

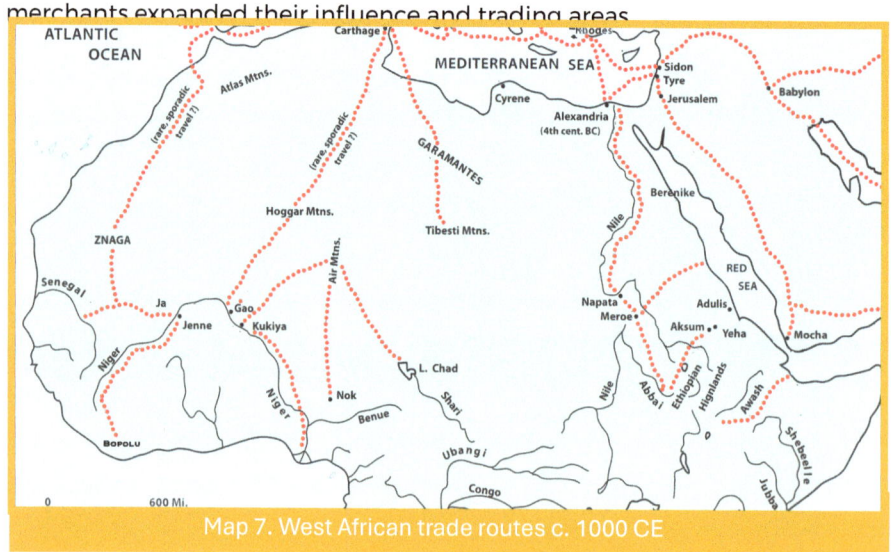

Map 7. West African trade routes c. 1000 CE

As with other regions of the world, trade in West Africa was characterized by competition and profit. But when rivalries pitted different traders against each other, those merchants often became embroiled in ethnic raids, reprisals, and outright wars.

In the middle of the new hierarchy were farmers and artisans. Non-farming families among the Mande, Wolof and Soninké were assigned to castes based on their skills. These **occupational castes** included metal smiths, potters, leatherworkers, iron smelters, and professional entertainers or griots. Occupational skills passed from parent to children, and no outsider could learn the skill or marry into the caste. The caste system for trades was rigid.

The New Hierarchy

At the top of new hierarchy was the political ruler who had nearly absolute political power. Descending from the first founding family no longer ensured political power. As war was used to settle political disputes, power came from those in control of the military. Power went to the best military strategist or the person who could mobilize an army. As horses were brought into Sahelian armies, horse riders were organized into **military cavalries**, which gave the army speed and increased the distance the army could travel.

West Africa was not alone in creating great empires. In Europe, the Roman Empire began in present-day Italy and spread through Europe, North African and the Middle East. In China, the Han created a massive empire which extended from Vietnam and Korea in the east to Afghanistan in the west. In the Middle East, Arabs founded the Ottoman Empire that stretched from the Persian Gulf in the east to Hungary in the northwest and from Egypt in the south to the Caucasus in the north. In South America, the Aztec and Incas founded powerful empires that lasted many centuries, until they were replaced by the Spanish Empire.

In many of those places, the state often seized land from the farmers and forced them to work on large-scale projects like the Great Wall of China or the Pyramids in Egypt. Along the Niger River, however, the state used its military, not farmers, to work on major projects.

A Seven-Year Drought

Between 700 CE and 1100 CE, rainfall dwindled, river levels fell, crops failed, and the Sahara expanded. A seven-year drought in the Soninké heartland caused havoc among the farming and herding communities. From the Gambia in the east all the way to Songhai in the west, people moved in search of water for themselves, their crops, and their herds. The heat and dryness of climate change was one factor that began driving people from the Sahel toward the forest belt.

Around 1076 CE, some Soninké traders from the **Dyula** caste moved from the town of **Kankaba** in present-day Mali to a town called **Kankan** in the Republic of Guinea. Dyula traders soon began exporting salt, kola, iron ore and other resources found in the forest areas. They were the first Mande-speakers many people in the forest belt encountered. As a result, the descendants of groups that earlier lived in the region often referred to all Mande traders as "Dyula" even centuries later.

Overtime, the Dyula were joined by Soninké ironsmiths, farmers or weavers. On the edge of the forest belt, they established their own small settlements. The first "strangers" would eventually host other Mande visitors. In those days, people lived closely together if they shared the same religion and ethnicity. For that reason, Muslims initially lived in a separate section of the main town, where they worshipped together.

These communities learned the language of those already living there, which helped to integrate the "strangers" into their new environment.

The Kono, Dama and Vai

The Dyula immigrants eventually splintered into three groups. Those who remained in the north became known as the **Kono.** A group that moved to the middle were called the **Dama**. Those who settled on the coast were known as the **Vai**.

According to Vai oral history, their ancestors migrated to the coast seeking the source of the Dei salt trade. They slowly traveled from **Kankan**, then to **Bopolu** before moving south toward **Cape Mount** in present-day Liberia.

In 1235 CE, another wave of Mande speakers moved to the region of what is now Liberia. This group came seeking sources of iron and hardwoods suitable for iron smelting. On the one hand, they were attracted to the area because of the iron-smelting activities of local groups, like the Kissi, and areas with large deposits of iron ore, like the **Putu Mountains.** On the other hand, supplies of both iron and hardwoods were becoming less available in the Sahel for Mande blacksmiths to use.

Over time, several factors caused tensions between Muslims and those who followed the Way of the Ancestors. First, some Islamic clerics began campaigns to convert non-Muslims. Second, Islamic law forbade Muslim women from marrying non-Muslim men, but it allowed Muslim men to marry women from other religions. Many non-Muslims saw that as unfair. Third, some Muslims resented the control of land by Poro leaders.

The peaceful approach of the Soninké was influenced by the teachings of Al-Hajj Salim Suwari. He taught Muslims that non-believers were not evil; their failure to follow Islam was to be accepted as the will of God. He assured Muslims that respecting the ways of nonbelievers was not against Islam. Al-Haj Suwari's teachings were adopted by the Dyula clan traders that first settled in the forest belt.

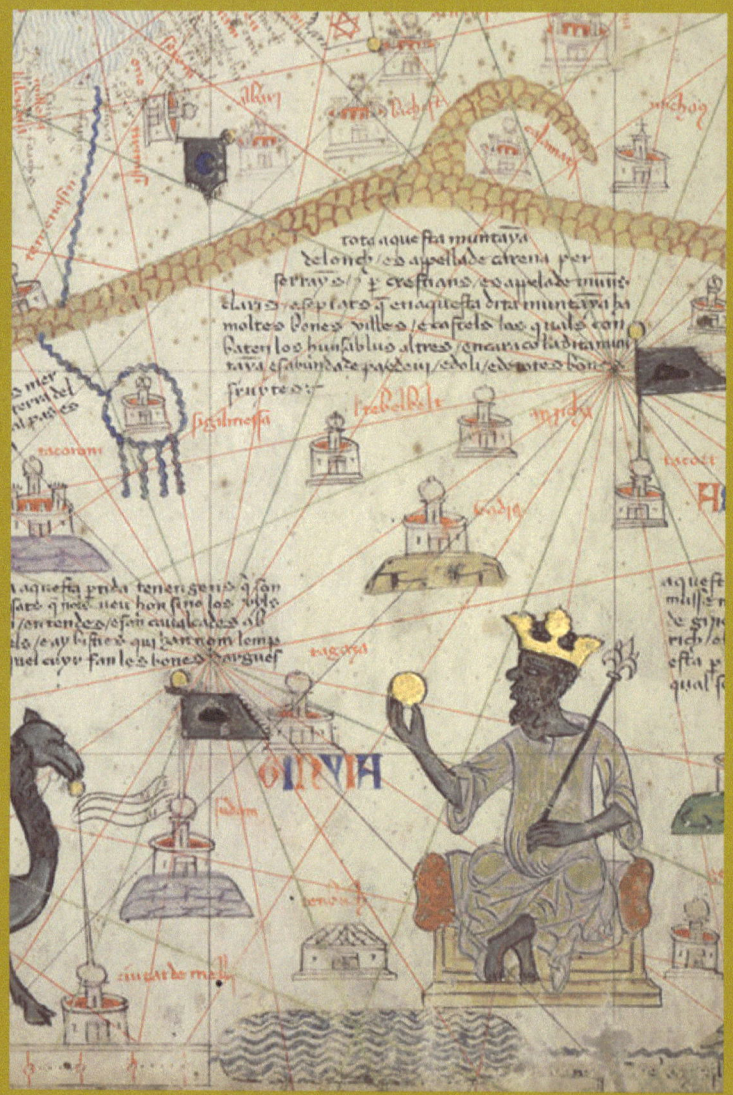

A map of West Africa drawn in 1375 CE by Abraham Cresques, a Jewish mapmaker from the island of Majorca. The man with the gold crown, gold staff and gold globe is **Mansa Musa of Mali**, as imagined by the artist.

Empires in the Sahel, 1230-1450 CE

Ghana apparently came into existence around 300 CE. The empire included many different Mande communities, but its core was the Soninké state of **Wagadugu**. At the height of Ghana's power, it controlled 100, 000 square miles between the Senegal and Niger Rivers. The word Ghana means *"warrior ruler,"* a title given to the highest official.

What we know about Ghana comes mainly from Arab writers. The empire was first mentioned in 830 CE by Muhammad ibn Musa al-Khwarizmi. In 1067 CE, it was included in a collection of stories from travelers to West Africa published by a scholar named **al-Bakr**i. According to the Arab writer **Al-Hamdani**, the empire's gold mines at Bambuk were the richest on earth.

Ghana's wealth derived mainly from the export of gold and salt. It remained West Africa's main trading center for 400 years, by tightly controlling information about two things: First, the sources of its gold and salt. Second, the routes that carried these commodities through its land.

Kumbi Saleh was the capital city of Ghana. The city was the main southern terminus of the Saharan trade routes, located on the edge of the Sahara. The empire's ruler lived in a section called **El-Ghaba**, which was protected by a stone wall. El-Ghaba functioned as the royal and spiritual capital of the Empire. It also contained a sacred grove of trees used for Soninké religious rites.

Beyond climate change, migrations were also driven by human-made factors. In Sahelian empires, several cultures and provinces shared one economy dominated by the trans-Saharan trade. Provinces and traders paid tributes and taxes which produced revenue for the government. In turn, rulers of the empires promised protection to traders and those living in the smaller provinces within its borders. They also standardized prices for goods and discouraged merchants from charging too much for their goods or paying farmers too little for their crops.

Ghana Declines

After 800 years of success, Ghana began to splinter for several reasons. First, its rulers and traders had focused only on trade with western North Africa, especially Morocco. They had ignored the developing markets to the east. Traders in the eastern part of West Africa opened new routes to alternative markets. By diverting traffic toward Egypt and beyond, they broke Ghana's monopoly on trade, wealth and power, which proved disastrous for the empire.

In addition, a seven-year drought forced the Soninké to migrate across West Africa in order to survive. Finally, Ghana collapsed after the Almoravid rulers of Morocco attacked between 1076-1077 CE, at a time the empire was too weak to defend itself.

After Ghana collapsed, several small states tried to fill the void left by the empire. To gain control of the

For more information, see these:

Azumah, John Alembillah. **The Legacy of Arab-Islam in Africa: A Quest for Inter-religious Dialogue** (Oxford: Oneworld, 2011).

Brooks, George E. "Ecological perspectives on Mande population movements, commercial networks, and settlement patterns from the Atlantic West Phase (ca. 5500-2500 B. C.) to the present," **History in Africa**, 16 (1989): 23-40.

Bühnen, Stephen. "Brothers, chiefdoms, and empires: On Jan Jansen's 'The representation of status in Mande'," **History in Africa**, Vol. 23 (1996): 111-120.

Johnson, Marion. "The cowrie currencies of West Africa," **Journal of African History**, XI (1970), Part 1: 17-49, Part 2: 331-353.

Johnson, Marion. "The nineteenth-century gold 'Mithqal.' in West and North Africa," **Journal of African History**, IX (1968): 547-569.

Levtzion, N. Ancient Ghana and Mali (London: Methuen, 1973).

Levtzion, N. and J. F. P. Hopkins, eds., **Corpus of Early Arabic Sources for West African History** (Princeton: Markus Wiener Publishers, 2011).

Levtzion, N. "The early states of the Western Sudan to 1500" (pp. 120-157), in J. F. Ade Ajayi and Michael Crowder, **History of West Africa**, Vol. I (New York: Columbia University Press, 1972).

Meillassoux, Claude. "The role of slavery in the economic and social history of Sahelo-Sudanic Africa," in J. E. Inikori, ed., **Forced Migration** (New York: Africana Publishing Co., 1982): 74-99.

Niane, D. T. **Recherches sur l'empire du Mali au Moyen Age** (Paris: Présence africaine, 1975).

Stewart, Marjorie Helen. "The role of the Manding in the hinterland trade of the Western Sudan: A linguistic and cultural analysis," **Bulletin de l'Institute francais d'Afrique noire**, Série B, 2 (1979): 218-302.

trade routes, they made alliances and warred with each other. Around 1140 CE, the Soso clan of **Kaniaga** began conquering the lands that had previously belonged to Ghana. By 1180 CE, it had even subjugated Wagadagu and forced the Soninké to pay tribute.

Ghana was eventually replaced by Kaniaga, a state created by the **Soso** and **Jalonké** peoples. In 1200 CE, the new empire covered half of present-day Guinea, along with parts of Sierra Leone, Senegal and Mali. Its ruler was **Sumaoro Kante**, also known as **Sumanguro**. He strongly opposed Islam and trade in enslaved Africans. He drew his support from blacksmiths and others traditional leaders.

Followers of Dankaran Tuman

Between 1200 and 1235 CE, Sumaoro Kante of the Soso people conquered nine states of the former Ghana Empire. He then turned his attention to capturing the Mandinka state of Mali. The defeated ruler of Mali, Dankaran Tuman, fled with his loyal soldiers and their families, together with other supporters. They journeyed to Kankan and from there down the **Milo River** and on to **Makona** to occupy the grasslands around **Kissidugu**, in present-day Guinea.

There were three routes from Kankan into the forest belt. One ran from that town to the Sierra Leone peninsula before ending at Cape Mount. A second route wound from **Musadu** to **Bopolu**, before reaching **Gowolo**, and finally Cape Mount. The third route, which was taken by the Soso, went south along the Milo River to the grasslands of northern Guinea around **Makona**.

Some of Dankaran Truman's followers were probably among the early ancestors of the Kpelle people. According to their oral traditions, some of their fore parents came from Mali and intermarried with people already living in the forest area. Those people included Kru speakers whom they met around **Nzérékoré**, Guinea, and the Dan in the east.

Some ancestors of the Loma, too, may have descended from the people fleeing Sumaoro's army because they share many similarities with the Kpelle. They first lived in the Beyla region of present-day Guinea, before founding Macenta. Once in the forest, all the southwest Mande groups began taking care of kola trees in cleared patches of forests near their villages. Both Loma and Kpelle staked claims to the kola trees using straw, pieces of calabash stuffed with cotton and other talismans.

Sumaoro of the Soso

After thirty-five years, a Mandinka region of Kaniaga called Mali rebelled against the empire. This rebellion was led by Sundiata Keita, who drew his support from Mali and Kangaba, the largest Malinké political units. His supporters included wealthy traders who had developed alternative trade routes to Arabia.

Keita's supporters were determined to spread Islam, a religion they had adopted. They also wanted to continue selling African captives along with gold.

In 1235 CE, Sundiata defeated Sumaoro. The victor launched West Africa's third major empire. Fearing violence, Sumaoro and his supporters fled to Futa Jalon before spreading towards the border of present-day Liberia. Many ethnic groups in Liberia today originated from those two migrations, including the Kpelle, Loma, Bandi and Mende.

Trade Routes and Towns

Migrants from the Sahel traveled along trade routes that linked the Niger to the salt-producing coast and the forest region of Liberia. These paths mainly passed through the town of Kankan, which was the main transit point for the flow of goods between the Bure goldmines on the one hand and the forest societies on the other.

There were other major trade towns along the forest edge in southern Guinea and northern Côte d'Ivoire. These were established well before the Mande migration. The Mande "strangers" found shelter in these towns by aligning with groups already living there.

Four major trade towns emerged near present-day day Liberia: **Kissidugu**, **Beyla**, **Musadu** and **Man**. Footpaths linked them together. These trade towns and others were located conveniently at the head of rivers and within 200 miles of the Atlantic Ocean. Each of the trading towns was at least five square miles, with around 3,000 residents.

This man is standing in an **archive** in present-day Mali. He is surrounded by really old written records. Those records were once kept in private homes. They are now housed in metal boxes to keep them safe.

Kissidugu, originally a Kissi town, became home to some Bandi, Mende, and Loma.

Beyla was likewise an ethnic melting pot. As early as 1200 CE, it was a **trading** station visited by Dyula merchants traveling down from the Niger River to buy kola and captives to be enslaved. From oral traditions, it seems likely that Kru-speakers or ancestors of the Ma founded it. The Loma who settled in the western section of the town joined the Kpelle who had settled in the eastern part.

Musadugu was the most legendary town in the region. As early as 1200 CE, it was a well-known stop on a trade route linking the forests to the Sahel. Ancestors of the Kpelle probably founded the town as a trading place. According to many oral traditions, the town once hosted some ancestors of the Gola, Loma, Kpelle, Kono, Bassa, Dan and Ma.

Another major trade town in the area was **Man**. It is located to the east in Côte d'Ivoire and inhabited by the Ma, Dan and Krahn. In earlier times, the ancestors of the Dan and Ma apparently lived in the area of Burkina Faso. According to linguistic studies, their languages closely resemble several small, isolated languages in Burkina Faso, northern Benin, and Western Nigeria. They have less in common with southwest Mande and northern Mande languages like Malinké and Vai.

All these trading towns hosted migrants on their way to the forests of Liberia, Sierra Leone and Cote d'Ivoire. The inhabitants of the towns welcomed the newcomers. Some of the migrants chose to make the towns their new homes, while others continued their journey south.

Where the Ruler Lives

In 1235 CE, Sundiata launched an empire that was larger and more prosperous than Ghana. The name was Mali, which means, *"Where the Ruler Resides."* Its ruler was given the title **Mansa.**

Much of what we know about the **Mali Empire** comes from the writings of Arab scholars, including Al-Umari, Abu-sa'id Uthman ad-Dukkali, Ibn Khaldun, and Ibn Battuta. The first writer to record the name of the empire as Mali was Ibn Battuta. Mansa Sundiata quickly formed a pact among the leading families of the Mandinka ethnic group. They seized control of the trade route running through **Adagh**.

To consolidate power, Sundiata suppressed the blacksmiths and other castes that had supported Sumaoro Kante. He also married a daughter of Ghana's last ruler. Sundiata then moved his capital south to **Niani**, which was close to the sources of gold, ivory, palm oil and salt. This location was also important for military reasons because it was away from the nomadic marauders of the Sahara.

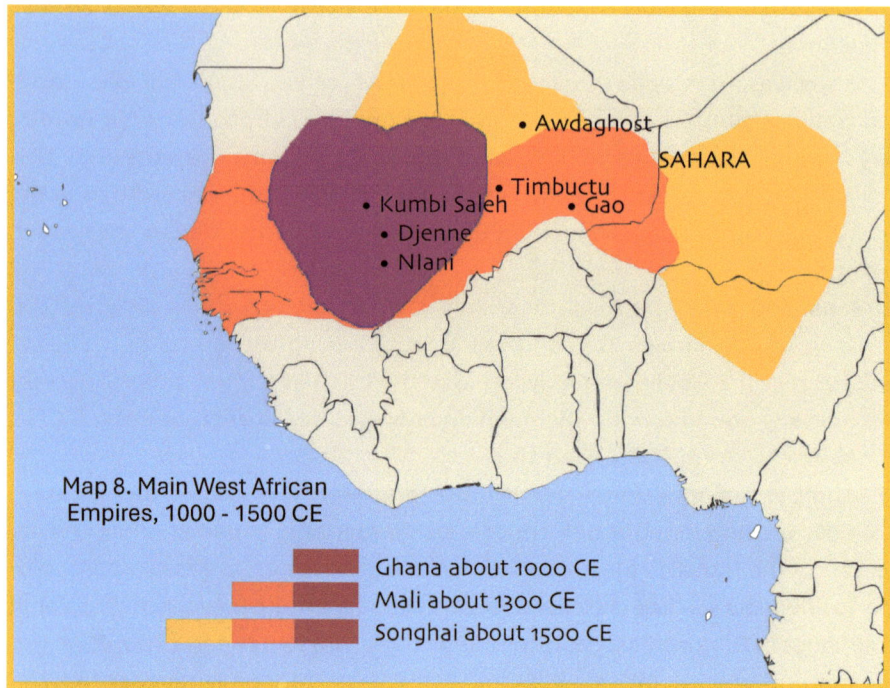

Map 8. Main West African Empires, 1000 - 1500 CE

Ghana about 1000 CE
Mali about 1300 CE
Songhai about 1500 CE

By the time of the Mali Empire, some political leaders and most traders had converted to this new "religion of the book." But conversion to Islam was gradual. Some who embraced Islamic prayer preferred local laws and political arrangements to Islamic ones. Many attended Friday prayers but practiced ancestor veneration and divination. Some adopted Arabic dress more as a sign of high status than religious affiliation.

Along with Islam, Middle Eastern traders brought the Arabic language to West Africa. Learning Arabic offered African merchants two advantages. First, Arabic gave them access to more markets because it was spoken from Spain through North Africa to Arabia. Second, it had a script that allowed the language to be written.

With the use of writing, governments could record payment of taxes. In addition, they could standardize currencies, weights and measures. Writing also enabled traders to keep their account books and enforce binding contracts.

Islamic teachers, called *Karamoko*, taught the Arabic language, writing, and the *Quran* (the holy book of Islam) to Muslim youth. Some Mande-speakers used Arabic script for divining and preparing amulets. Even in non-Muslim area of West Africa, local people viewed Arabic writing with respect, and some rulers hired Islamic clerics as secretaries.

By using Arabic writing, the rulers of West African empires were able to access knowledge in books, keep permanent records, and send written messages

Great Mosque of Timbuktu

halfway around the world. Access to writing skills offered Sahelian empires decisive advantages over non-literate forest societies.

At the height of Mali's power, it was 1,200 miles wide. It included parts of the Sahara, Sahel, savannah, and the coast between Gambia and the Rio Grande Rivers of present-day Guinea Bissau. Most of the empire's people were farmers, but it included nomads, cattle herders, artisans, and fishermen. Near its eastern border was the salt-mining town of **Maghaza**, which had a mosque built entirely of salt. Mali's borders were defended by an army of 100,000 strong, among whom were 10,000 men on horses.

Crossing the Atlantic Ocean?

After Sundiata's death, seven other mansas ruled Mali. But they were insignificant compared to the ninth mansa, Abubukari II. According to Egyptian scholar Al-Umari, Mansa Abubukari II in 1310 CE sent 200 ships with men and supplies to find what lay beyond the Atlantic Ocean. Only one ship returned. Its captain reported that he had turned back when he saw the other ships disappearing into the wild ocean.

Mansa Abubukari II was not happy with this report, so he decided to lead another expedition. He ordered the building of 1,000 ships off the coast of Senegambia. In 1311 CE, he resigned as ruler and sailed away with doctors, navigators, sailors and religious men. Every ship had a supply ship attached to it with enough food to last his men two years. The ships reportedly entered the Canary

Current, a river in the ocean powerful enough to take vessels to the Americas.

No one knows what happened to the explorers because Mansa Abubukari II never returned home. He was replaced by Musa, Sundiata's nephew.

Around 1250 CE, Sundiata seized control of **Timbuktu**, a town established by the **Sanhaja Berbers**. Under his control, the town became internationally renowned as a commercial center and a seat of Islamic learning.

The University of Timbuktu and its libraries attracted scholars from throughout the Muslim world to study, write, and teach. Courses offered by the university included mathematics, geography, history, astronomy, chemistry, and Islamic studies. A devout Muslim, Mansa Musa funded the building of a great mosque, which was unrivaled in West Africa.

Djenné, another city on the Niger River, became the hub for the export of gold to Europe and the Arab world from the Akan forest in present-day Republic of Ghana. Djenné, too, became a center of Islamic scholarship and boasted of its own Great Mosque. It was the southern terminus for goods that had passed through Timbuktu, such as salt, gold and kidnapped Africans who would be sold into slavery.

The Mandinka were the core of Mali. For that reason, the Manding language became the language of trade throughout West Africa, just as English arose as a trade language at a later time. Many non-Mande speakers adopted the dominant language to gain access to wider knowledge and privileges.

The World's Gold Supplier

In 1326 CE, Mali achieved notoriety in the Mediterranean world when Mansa Musa undertook his first *hajj*. This trip to Mecca in Saudi Arabia is required of all Muslim adults who can afford it and are physically fit. The mansa crossed the Sahara with gold ore loaded on 100 camels. His traveling party included thousands of enslaved persons and soldiers, as well as officials and their wives. The entourage bartered in the bazaars of Cairo using so much gold that its value fell in Egypt.

Between 1350 CE and 1450 CE, the Mali Empire reached the peak of its power and grandeur. During that period, it exported enough gold to Europe and Arabia that it eventually provided almost two-thirds of the world's supply of gold.

New Ideas and Information

One positive outcome of the trans-Saharan trade was the growth of trading towns along the Niger River. The river begins in Futa Jalon in Guinea and flows north through the heart of West Africa before turning south and exiting into the Gulf of Guinea in the Atlantic Ocean. Towns in this valley grew where trade routes intersected. Towns like Timbuktu, Gao, Djenné and Bamako were at the heart of the Mali and Songhai empires between 1200 CE and 1500 CE. In those places, merchants of the Sahara traded with those of the Sahel.

Traders living in these towns profited from the markets they organized. But the towns and their population also benefited; they gained access to foreign goods, as well as new ideas about history, philosophy, medicine and other subjects, Great profits led to large new buildings, and new knowledge led to the establishment of libraries and universities, which attracted scholars from near and far.

Selling Africans to the Middle East

International trade took a tragic turn when African traders begin kidnapping fellow Africans, whom they exported to the Mediterranean and Middle East, where they would be enslaved.

Slavery, which involved forcing people to work for free, existed in many parts of the world. Africa had slavery on a small scale before Arabs and Europeans came. Back then, enslaved persons in Africa were usually held as payment for debt or seized as prisoners of war. But they could egain their freedom and rejoin their communities.

The practice of enslaving West Africans on a large scale began in 800 CE after the Arabs seized Egypt and occupied Nubia in Eastern Africa. They forced Nubia to sign a *baqt* or contract to provide 360 captives a year, a contract that remained in force for 500 years. Between 700 CE and 1900 CE an estimated nine million enslaved West Africans labored in the Mediterranean area.

The hunt for African captives caused many deaths. Some died when slave catchers raided their towns. Others perished while crossing the Sahara. Captives would walk for days or even weeks. Guards would whip any captives who walked slowly or resisted. If someone was too weak or ill to walk quickly, guards would leave them to die.

Most survivors spent their lives as servants to merchants and rich families. Some served as soldiers in Arab armies. Based on exceptional service, a few enslaved Africans rose to become sheikhs, sultans, and merchants.

A demand for cheap labor increased in the Middle East mainly due to the growing of sugar cane on plantations. Sugar-cane farming started in New Guinea, then spread to Philippines, Indonesia, and India before reaching Arabia and Europe. After being pioneered in Lebanon, growing sugar on plantations was adopted by many Mediterranean countries. On these plantations, Africans quickly outnumbered enslaved people from other regions.

A **compass**, writing **quill** and **map** with an **arrow** pointing to the area now known as Liberia.

World Turned Upside Down, 1462-1591 CE

On August 15, 1462 CE, the first Europeans visited the area of present-day Liberia. They were Portuguese sailors led by Captain **Pedro de Sintra** who first stopped near Cape Mesurado. One of their goals was to find the source of malagueta spice, which was rare and valuable in their homeland. About 40 years after this visit, a record of de Sintra's travels was published by Alvise de Ca da Mosto, a sailor. He used de Sintra's notes and oral sources to write his account.

According to Ca da Mosto, one night after de Sintra and his men arrived they saw, *"many fires among* the trees and along the shore." Sailing 16 miles further down the coast toward the Junk River, they saw "A great forest of very green trees which grow right down to the water's edge."

When three local men from aboard a canoe climbed onto the ship, the Portuguese tried to kidnap them. Two jumped into the ocean, but one was captured and taken away to Portugal. That was the first of many kidnappings of local people by European visitors.

De Sintra's voyage was sponsored by Prince Henry of Portugal. In 1415 CE, he had fought in North Africa, alongside his father King Joao I. In that battle, Portuguese troops captured **Ceuta** from Morocco, a town that had been the center of the gold trading and coin minting for 500 years.

While there, they discovered a closely guarded secret. According to Arab traders, gold and kidnapped Africans were being traded for beads and other trinkets in Timbuktu, a city in the heart of West Africa. The merchants also said the gold came from vast mines further south. To find those gold fields, the Portuguese decided to send ships around the coast of West Africa. No Europeans had previously sailed beyond **Cape Bojador**.

Prince Henry was next in line to replace his father as the king, but left the royal court after 1420 CE to pursue commercial and religious interests. He moved to **Sagres**, a town that attracted sailors from across the Mediterranean world. It was a center of navigation, shipbuilding and mapmaking. Henry's home became a meeting place where people interested in sailing came to learn from each other. For that reason, historians credit Prince Henry with initiating the **"Age of European Discoveries."**

Portuguese Caravels

One of the first tasks faced by Henry and his team was to build a ship suitable for the voyages along the West African coast. Traditional European ships were too heavy and slow for long-distance travel. Borrowing from Chinese and Arab ship designs, Prince Henry and his team created the caravel, a new style of ship. It was light and had a shallow bottom, but with a large cargo area to store supplies for long voyages. Caravel sails were triangular, allowing the ship to turn quicker than others.

Prince Henry launched several other voyages to West Africa. De Sintra was followed to West Africa by other Portuguese navigators, including **Alvise Ca da Mosto**, **Duarte Pacheco**

For more information, see these:

Blake, John W., ed., ***Europeans in West Africa, 1450-1560***, Second Series, LXXXVI (London: The Haklyut Society, 1941-42).

Cissoko, S. M. "The Songhay from the twelfth to the sixteenth century," ***General History of Africa: Africa from the Twelfth to the Sixteenth Century***, Vol. IV. Berkeley: University of California Press, 1992).

de Cintra, Piedro. "Voyages to the coasts and islands of Africa, in John Green, ***A New General Collection of Voyages and Travels***, Vol. 1 (London: Thomas Astley, 1745-1747).

Elbl, Ivana. "Man of his time (and peers): A new look at Henry the Navigator," ***Luso-Brazilian Review***, Vol. XXVIII, No. 2 (1991): 73-89.

Epstein, Stephen A. ***Genoa & the Genoese, 958-1528*** (Chapel Hill: University of North Carolina, 1996).

Kupperman, Karen Ordahl, ***The Atlantic in World History*** (New York: Oxford University Press, 2012).

Ly-Tall, M. "The decline of the empire of Mali: the fifteenth to sixteenth centuries," ***General History of Africa: Africa from the Seventh to the Eleventh Century***, Vol. IV. Berkeley: University of California Press, 1992).

Newitt, Malyn. ***A History of Portuguese Overseas Expansion, 1400-1668*** (London: Routledge, 2005).

Periera, Duarte Pacheco. ***Esmeraldo de Situ Orbis***, translated by George H. T. Kimble (London: The Hakluyt Society, 1937; written c. 1505-1508).

Russell, Peter. ***Prince Henry 'the Navigator': A Life*** (New Haven, Conn.: Yale University Press, 2000).

Vilar, Pierre. ***A History of Gold and Money, 1450-1920*** (London: Verso, 1984).

Pereira and **Fernao Gomes**. They came seeking the source of malagueta, gold, African captives, and a sea route to Asia.

Portuguese began trading with West Africans and soon established their own towns in the region. Their arrival caused a radical change in the direction of trade. Merchants who previously took goods to the Sahel now brought them to the coast. That shift soon overturned the social, political, and economic structure of the region. Although Prince Henry died in 1460 CE, his legacy continued.

Beyond a search for riches, Prince Henry wanted to block the further expansion of Islam in West Africa. Muslim North Africans from Morocco had earlier conquered Gibraltar, most of Spain, Portugal, and southern France. The people of those countries remained intolerant of Islam and Judaism for centuries.

Beginning in 1299 CE, Muslims conquered another vast territory. The Ottoman Empire spread from Turkey to embrace Western Asia, the Caucasus, North Africa, and the Horn of Africa. In 1453 CE, its government blocked Asian spices, silk cloths and other goods from reaching Europe. This spurred Europeans to seek routes to Asia that bypassed Muslim lands.

Accounts of European Visitors

After de Sintra, other Portuguese visitors soon visited Cape Mount, Cape Mesurado, and the Cestos River. They rarely went into the interior. Their writings

A Portuguese **caravel**

focused almost exclusively on coastal trade. As a result, early Portuguese visitors left very little firsthand information on the life of people in the area.

Writing in 1505 CE, Duarte Pacheco Pereira left one of the earliest Portuguese accounts of the area around Liberia. He reported that residents of a place called **Coya**, beyond present-day Freetown, exchanged 23-carat gold for sea salt. He said Coya was located 104 miles up the Mano River. According to Pereira, regular visitors to Freetown included Soso traders, who traveled in caravans of up to 2,000 men. They traded with the **Sape** and other people living along the coast.

As Portuguese visits increased, words from their language were adopted by local people. A few examples are "dash," "palava," and "cestos," which mean gift, discussion, and baskets. In addition, some names given to local rivers and geographical landmarks by the Portuguese are still used, including Cape Mount, Cape Mesurado, Cape Palmas, River Cess and St. Paul River.

The Renegade Joao Afonso

In 1533 CE, one of the first ships not approved by the Portuguese government reached Cape Mount. The captain was a Portuguese **outlaw** named **Joao Afonso**, who traded for gold and ivory. He reported meeting Klao people somewhere between River Cess and Cape Mesurado, where he bought malagueta spice.

Around the same time, an English captain named **William Hawkins** visited River Cess. He bartered there for ivory. To avoid the powerful Portuguese, English ships limited their trade to the coast from the Cestos River to Mina in present-day Ghana.

Cholera and Measles Arrive

Another English visitor to the Liberian coast was **John Lok**. In 1554, he led a fleet of three ships from southern England. Lok left a slightly more detailed account than Hawkins. He recorded the names of several towns between River Cess and Cape Palmas, including Cakeado, Shawgro, Shyawe or Shavo and Croke. He described Cape Palmas as, "A fair high land, some low parts of which by the waterside seem red cliffs, with white streaks like highways."

Aboard one of his ships was the London merchant **William Towerson**. In 1555, Towerson returned to West Africa with two ships. His journey from southern England to River Cess took two months. According to Towerson, the area between River Cess and Cape Palmas grew the most malagueta. In one day at River Cess, he exchanged basins, bracelets and beads for 1,100 pounds of malagueta and two ivory tusks.

Towerson described both women and men carving items out of the bark of trees. He also witnessed blacksmiths making javelin heads, boat-making tools, and various other iron objects. He recorded a few local phrases along with their translations that he heard while trading.

In 1626, a Dutch fleet came to Cape Mount. Its visit was disastrous for residents. The Dutch sailors unintentionally brought cholera. Measles came soon after. Those two diseases did not exist locally, so people in Cape Mount had no immunity to them. As a result, cholera and measles together "swept away the best part of the people."

The Thaba, Marie and the Dutchman

In 1620, **Samuel Brun** of Switzerland also visited Cape Mount. He met several Dutch sailors who were living among the Vai. They had survived a shipwreck one year before. According to Brun, a few local people spoke Portuguese. The *thaba* (meaning ruler) spoke French, and his wife, "Marie," spoke "good Dutch." A native of Cameroon, Marie had learned Dutch from her previous husband, a Dutch trader. Six years before Brun's visit, the Dutchman was killed while fighting for the *thaba*, who quickly married Marie.

According to European visitors, the rulers of Cape Mount throughout the 1600s had similar sounding names. They were identified as *"Farambo-rey," "Faran bure," "Frambore," "Flam-bourre," and "Falm Burre."* Despite different spellings, their names all sound like the Cape Mount family now known as *"Fahnbulleh."*

Mali Declines

After 200 years of success, the Mali Empire began declining in the 1400s CE for several reasons. First, European traders were increasingly getting goods from coastal communities that had flowed to the Sahel. Second, the

> **Popular foreign goods from Sierra Leone to Elmina, 1558**
>
> **Clothing**: cloaks or overcoats, gowns, hats, cheap gloves, leather bags
>
> **Containers**: basins of various sorts, but mainly brass or bronze, pots of course tin that hold a quart or more, Dutch kettles with brass handles, large engraved brass basins, large engraved pewter basins and pitchers, large basins used for bathing, Dutch basins, red cans
>
> **Fabrics**: linen cloth, cheap red cloth, coarse French coverlet, packing sheets, Spanish blankets
>
> **Furniture**: small Flemish locked boxes, cheap chests
>
> **Tools**: cheap knives, large pins, wedges of iron, horse nails, axe heads hammers, short pieces of iron
>
> **Jewelry**: brass bracelets, lead bracelets, cheap beads, blue corals, small bells
>
> **Weapons**: swords, daggers
>
> Plus "any other trifling articles you will"

rulers of Mali lost their unity; they disagreed on who would replace them. Third, provinces of the empire wanted more control over the salt and gold trade. Those problems led provinces to break away.

Living on the Atlantic coast, the **Wolof** in present-day Senegal had access to goods from European traders. In the early 1400s CE, they were the first people to leave Mali's orbit. Mali's problems increased in 1430 CE, when the Tuareg seized Timbuktu, the richest city in the empire. Finally, the empire's fate was sealed by a rebellion in Gao, a wealthy city founded in 800 CE.

Gao was the capital of Songhai, one of Mali's richest provinces. In the 1430s CE, Sonni Ali Ber led Songhai's rise to become an empire. He quickly took control of important trans-Saharan trade routes, as well as other cities and provinces. Although a Muslim, he protected those who followed the Way of the Ancestors from forced conversion to Islam.

The Great Mosque of Gao

Sonni was succeeded by **Mohamed Toure** (1443-1538), a military commander. Under Toure, trade increased with Europe and Asia. He also standardized weights, measures, and the currency. During Toure's reign, Gao attracted scholars and skilled workers from Arabia, Egypt, Morocco, and Muslim Spain. He strengthened political and cultural ties with many Muslim countries by exchanging ambassadors with them.

During Toure's reign, Songhai stretched from present-day Senegal and Gambia to what is now northwest Nigeria and central Niger. Based on his many achievements, he earned the title "Askia the Great."

Around 1510, a Great Mosque Complex was built in the center of Gao. It contained two prayer halls, one for men and one for women. A wall surrounded the mosque and the grave of Askiya Mohammed. His tomb is a large stepped pyramid built of mud bricks and mud plaster.

Under **Askia the Great**, religious tensions flaired when Songhai rulers sought to impose Islamic laws on everyone. They launched a *jihad* against those who followed the Way of the Ancestors, many of whom were not Malinké or Songhai. Those rules included segregation of men from women in public gatherings, "proper" dressing for women, an end to fortune telling, and a ban on non-Islamic amulets.

After **Askiya Toure** died in 1528, several less-powerful rulers followed. Cities like Gao, Timbuktu, and Djenne continued to flourish based on wealth from gold, salt and African captives sold into slavery. But a civil war broke out in 1591. During that time of internal weakness, Ahmad I al-Mansur Saadi, the Sultan of Morocco, launched an attack. His troops conquered Songhai and seized the routes to the West African goldfields. Chaos in the Sahel unleashed dislocation throughout West Africa.

Upheaval in the Region

Before 1560 CE, 90 percent of the present-day Liberian forested land was uninhabited. The ancestors of southwest Mande, southeast Mande and the Dyula were living in the savannah. The town known as Kissidugu laid at the heart of Kissi territory. The Gola were living in a place now called Mana, which is north of Bopolu. Along the coast near riverbanks were a few Kru groups, like the Dei and Klao.

Those groups were joined after 1235 by the ancestors of the Kpelle, Loma, Mende and Bandi. According to various oral traditions, many ethnic groups now living in the northwest met the Gola, Kissi and Dei when they arrived. Their migrations from the Sahel to the savannah was sparked by two big events: The defeat of Mali ruler Dankaran Tuman, followed by the ouster of Soso leader Sumaoro Kante.

According to Kpelle history, the town now known as **Musadugu** was founded by one of their ancestors, an herbalist. Some Loma ancestors first settled around Musadugu. But the town later became the Kpelle capital, just as Macenta emerged as the key trade town in Loma territory.

Sundiata, who seized control of Mali from Sumanguru, was strongly supported by Faran of the Kamara clan. After Sundiata consolidated control over Mali, the Kamara clan began a massive expansion around **Niani** in present-day Guinea.

The **Mandinka**, also known as **Mandingo**, were the core of the Mali Empire. Clans from that group had earlier drifted south attracted by the trade in forest goods. As their empire declined, larger and much more aggressive Mandinka clans invaded coastal areas from Senegambia to the Gold Coast. They had access to horses, advanced technologies, use of writing, and knowledge of Arabic, which was an international language. Those assets gave them military, economic, and political advantages over other groups.

According to the oral histories of several ethnic groups, Faran's descendants led a large Malinké migration to Musadu around 1550 CE. During that time, most ancestors of Liberians were living near six major trade towns in Guinea: Musadu, Kissidougou, Macenta, Missadugu, and Nzérékoré. As these towns had grown, they attracted commerce from many groups in the area, as well as Dyula traders from the Sahel.

The Kamara clan settled in **Musadugu** and areas further south. Foningama, also of the Kamara clan, ruled over the town sometime in the late 1500s. That historic town is now the religious center of the Kamara Clan.

Loma oral traditions recall an agreement between their ancestors and Faran Kamara called the ***kokologi***. Both sides pledged to "avoid warfare and to respect the traditions and customs of the original inhabitants, in particular their sacred sites." Malinké oral traditions also acknowledge the existence of the "laws" in the Konyan region of Guinea that protected trading and traditional practices.

Five "War Houses"

The kokologi was overturned when members of five Malinké families arrived in the forest belt after the collapse of the Mali Empire. Descendants of the Kieta, Kamara, Kouranko, Konionké, and Diomanké clans were known in Malinké as **sanangui**, meaning "war houses."

These five families all had strong ties to power and privilege in the Mali Empire. Beginning around 1500 CE, they secured control of key trade towns in southern Guinea. It is possible to estimate the time and routes of their migrations by piecing together oral traditions and linguistic evidence. They first occupied areas around Kissidugu, Musadugu and Macenta in the west, Missadougou and Nzérékoré in the middle and Man in the east.

Large numbers of the Kamara clan first settled in the northern-most region of what is now the Republic of Guinea above the Makona River. But they moved into what is now called Lofa County between 1500 CE and 1600 CE. The **Kourankos** moved from Koinadougou near **Segou** in Mali down to **Macenta**, deep in Loma territory. The **Kieta clan**, who were relatives of Sundiata, moved to the

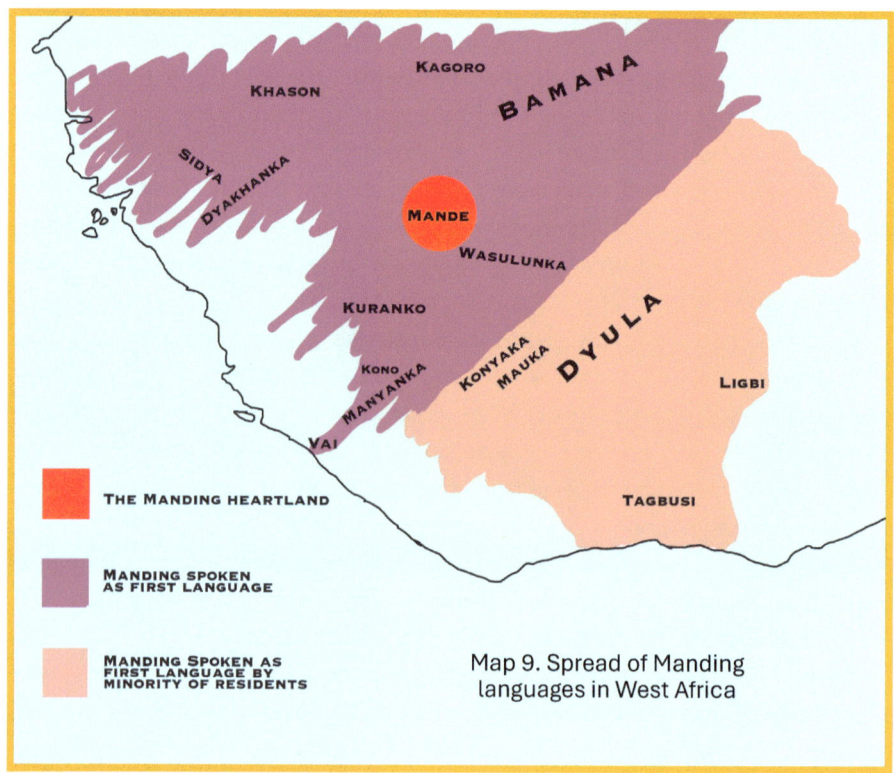

Map 9. Spread of Manding languages in West Africa

northern end of **Kissidugu**, Guinea. As the Mandinka moved toward the Sierra Leone peninsula, they pushed some Kissi from Kissidugu to Foya in former Bandi territory and Kailahun in Sierra Leone. Those two places are roughly 85 miles from Kissidugu. Liberian Kissi's oral history says that they migrated to western Liberia by crossing the Makonna River from their previous home in Guinea. They say their move was spurred by a hunter's search for wild game.

Many towns in Liberia now occupied by the Kissi were originally Bandi towns and still have Bandi names, like Kelema, Kolblama and Vabalahuu. This suggests a cascading displacement of people, including the Kono who relocated to present-day Sierra Leone.

According to Bandi oral traditions, their ancestors migrated from a town called Korblima, Guinea, in search of fertile farmland in northwest Liberia. The Bandi groups included blacksmiths and professional entertainers. Their oral traditions point to Mandinka salt and slave traders teaching them the art of cotton cloth weaving.

Mende oral traditions claim their ancestors came into present-day Liberia and Sierra Leone to enter the growing coastal salt-trade. Written records suggest they served as troops in the Mane invasion.

Loma Contract with Mandinka

As the Mandinka pushed south, they forced some ancestors of the Kissi, Loma, Mende and Bandi from Guinea into what is now Liberia. Trouble began when some Mandinka sought to eradicate the Way of the Ancestors and convert everyone to Islam. In doing this, the northern Mande "strangers" had violated the original *kokologi* agreement. The result was a large-scale Loma migration from Guinea to present-day Liberia.

According to Loma oral history, their ancestors moved to Liberia seeking wild game, fertile land, and refuge from religious persecution. They apparently followed the St. Paul River into Liberia, where they founded Zigida and five other towns in Zorzor district: Woniguomai, Gissimai, Wobormai, Wolorballah and Zieyema. The Loma in Liberia were pushed about 190 miles from Macenta.

Many Mandinka groups led by horse-riding warriors repeatedly invaded the forest belt for three reasons: First, they were fleeing the Moroccan troops who had conquered Mali. Second, they were seeking new lands where they could settle their families and farmers. Third, their rulers wanted to wrest control of the European trade from Atlantic, Kru and Southern Mande speakers.

Mandinka fighters on horses

Mane Fighters Attack the Coast, 1540-1563 CE

The next phase of the Mandinka expansion, known as the Mane invasion, first focused on seizing the Bullom territory in present-day Sierra Leone. A key source on those events was **Andre Alvares de Almada**, a Portuguese merchant who recorded oral accounts 30 years later.

It was apparently launched around 1560 CE from the area above Kissidugu by the children and grandchildren of the Kamara clan who came from Mali between 1495 and 1505 CE. Having lived in the region for two generations, they were able to recruit Mende, Bandi and Kissi fighters in their quest to wrest control of the European trade from coastal residents.

Almada identified a people called **Sape** along the coast from Cap Verga in Guinea to Sherbro Island. They were the ancestors of the Temne, Bullom, Bom, and Kim. Their languages belong to the **Atlantic family**. Related languages were spoken by the Baga, Landuma, and Monan in Guinea, as well as the Kissi and Gola in Liberia.

When the Mane entered Sape territory along the coast, "they understood each other," Almada said. This claim can be interpreted in two ways. On the one hand, it is likely the common people among the Sape understood Mane fighters who spoke Atlantic languages. On the other hand, it is possible the Sape and Mane rulers both spoke Malinké. After all, there had been several previous Mandinka incursions along the coast over centuries.

In the land of the Sapes, there were sugar cane, cotton, malagueta spice, white rice, white corn, wax, ivory and kola. Animals included elephants, leopards, buffalo and deer. But cows were brought from a distance by Fula herders.

One animal unique to this region was the chimpanzee. According to Almada, it was clever, walked on two legs, and lacked a tail. If raised by people from young, chimpanzees would fetch water from a creek and bring it in a pot on their heads. They also learned to pound foodstuff in a mortar. Their hairy bodies were mainly what made them look different from people.

According to Almada, the area around today's Freetown was once seen as the jewel of Guinea. During his time, "Guinea" was often defined as the coast between Dakar and Cape Mount. Sape people were prosperous, peaceful and happy, he said. Two groups, called **Putaze** and **Souze** by Almada, frequently came from the interior highlands to this coast. They would bring cloths, ready-made clothes and dyes to exchange for salt. But the trade was driven away by the Mane invasion.

"Kingdom" of the Sape

Almada often referred to the kingdom of the Sape. Many European writers mentioned other "kingdoms" in West Africa, which often confused readers into thinking African governments were copies of those elsewhere. But "kingdom" had more than

For more information, see these:

Béavogui, Facinet. *Les Toma (Guineé et Liberia) au temps des négriers et de la colonization from gaise* (Paris: L'Hamattan, 2001).

Bühnen, Stephen. "In quest of Susu," *History in Africa*, Vol. 21 (1994): 1-47.

d'Azevedo, Warren L. "Some historical problems in the delineation of a Central West Atlantic Region," *Annals of the New York Academy of Science*. Vol. 96 (January 1962): 512-538.

de Almada, André 'Alvares. *Brief Treatise on the Rivers of Guinea, Part I: Translated Text*. Translated with annotations by Paul E. H. Hair ([S. I.]: Andreas Heuijerjans, 2010).

Dornelas, André. *An Account of Sierra Leone and the Rivers of Guinea of Cape Verde* (Lisboa: Junta de Investigaçöes Cientificas do Ultramar, 1977).

Geysbeek, Tim. History from the Musadu epic. Ph. D. dissertation, Michigan State University, 2002.

Kerr, Robeert. *A General History and Collection of Voyages and Travels*, Vol. VII (London: T. Cabell, 1824).

Massing, Andreas W. "The Mane, the decline of Mali and Mandinka expansion towards the South Windward Coast," *Cahiers d'Études africaines*, 97, 26 (1985): 21-55.

Person, Yves. "Ethnic movements and acculturation in Upper Guinea since the fifteenth century," *African Historical Studies*, IV, 3 (1971): 669-689.

Rodney, Walter A. *A History of the Upper Guinea Coast, 1545-1800* (Oxford: Clarendon Press, 1980).

Weisswange, Karin "Feindshaft und Verwandtshaft: Konflikt und Kooperation in Zusammenleben von Loma und Mandingo in dem Ort Bobrkeza in Liberie," M. A. thesis, Johan Wolfgang Goethe-Universität, Frankfurt, 1969).

one meaning in earlier times. Almada did not mean that the Sape were unified under a single ruler, which he explained several times. Instead, he used "**kingdom**" to describe people who shared similarities in language and culture.

Almada cited several cultural practices that were common to Atlantic-language groups. For example, both men and women filed their top and bottom **front teeth** to enhance beauty.

Another common pattern was their ritual for welcoming guests. After explaining the reason for their visit, guests were given hot bath water and fresh clothes. Once visitors were refreshed and dressed, they would be taken to meet the head of the home and then given a meal. Important male guests, including traders, would sometimes be offered a temporary local wife. If she gave birth later, her child would be raised as a family member by the host – with one exception: The child of a European guest would be given to the father!

A third shared practice was their system of justice. Trials were held in a round hall decorated with finely-colored mats. The ruler and the leading men, called *soleteguis*, would sit together. The advocate for each side would appear wearing masks and decorated with feathers and bells. They would take turns speaking until they had completed their arguments. The ruler and his ***soleteguis*** would then deliver their verdict.

If a consensus verdict was not possible, **guilt** would be discovered by applying heat to the suspects. Whoever was scalded was judged to be guilty. Civil cases required the payment of fines. But in criminal cases, the guilty party would often be killed or sold into slavery.

When a ruler died, Atlantic-language groups installed his replacement in a similar way. After the **funeral**, the leaders would rush to the house of the successor. He would be tied up and given several lashes with a whip. Afterwards, they would calmly wash him before dressing him in the official robe, shirt, pants, and red cap. Everyone would then assemble at the palava hut to hear a speech by the oldest leader. After the speech, the new ruler was given the *queto*, a weapon used to behead criminals. As long as he held power, he would carry that axe as a sign of his office.

In addition, *soleteguis* were also elevated in similar ways across local cultures. A goat would be killed and its upper organs brought to the ruler, including the heart and liver. In a ceremony at the palava hunt, he would smear goat blood on the cheeks, hands, and feet of persons scheduled for elevation. He would then throw rice flour over the blood and put a red cap on their heads. Men who went through this ceremony would be treated with respect even by other ethnic groups.

According to Almada, each funeral was preceded by a wake in the town center where food and drinks were served. The deceased were buried in clothes and, when possible, in gold jewelry, including earrings, nose rings, and bracelets. Former rulers were buried along a road outside the town. Above their graves, villagers would erect a house of straw.

Two Key Rituals

Almada was one of the first Europeans to write about two sacred local rituals. The first involved a visit to town by a **masked dancer** which he called the "devil." In the Way of the Ancestors tradition, it was known as "the forest thing." Before its arrival, residents rushed to hide non-initiates behind closed doors. Almada said the entourage consisted of the ruler and other leaders. He claimed they "go around naked," while playing a "hollowed-out stick like a blow pipe." During the ceremony, no one indoors was allowed to make a sound. According to Almada, anyone who did would be handed over to the entourage to be killed.

A second event was the **rite** that marked the elevation of girls to women. For one year or more, all the girls from the community were sent to a large, isolated house which Almada called "the House of Religion." During their isolation from family and friends, the girls were given new names and treated as "nuns." Their guardian was "an old noble" regarded as a "good-living man." When the girls emerged, they were decked in jewelry, decorations and fine clothes. Near the center of the town, the girls danced to a symphony of large and small drums, all playing in harmony. Suitors flocked to these dances to request permission from fathers to marry their daughters.

According to Almada, the Sape were not as "warlike" as those groups north of the Grand River at Biguba in present-day Guinea-Bissau. For that reason, they could not defend themselves in organized ways. To make matters worse, neighbors would not offer help when another group was attacked. That was why, Almada said, the Mane invaders easily subdued local people. Two exceptions were the **Limba** and **Jalunga**. When attacked, both hid in **underground shelters** until their enemies retreated.

Knee-Length Smocks and Short Arrows

Almada was born on the Portuguese-controlled island of Santiago off the coast of Senegambia. He had traveled extensively in West Africa. He was convinced that the Mane leaders were Mandinka for several reasons. Their speech, their dress, and their weapons all resembled those of Mandinkas he had seen elsewhere.

Almada previously saw Mandinka men dressed in two unique items of cotton like the Mane. One was a **knee-length smock** with wide sleeves that stopped at the elbow. Their pant legs were wide and the crotch reached below their knees. They also wore bird **feathers** of different colors in their caps and on their shirts.

Almada said most West Africans used long bows and long arrows. But the Mane, like the Mandinka, carried small bows and short arrows. That style difference gave them an advantage on the battlefield. They could reuse the long arrows of their enemies. But their opponents could not shoot short arrows from their long bows! In addition, the Mane coated the tips of their arrows with a highly **poisonous sap** from a tree that others didn't use.

"More Force and Fiercely Than Ever"

Some local people told Almada that the Mandinka had attacked the area many times over centuries. But the Manes had invaded with "more force and ferocity than ever seen in any nation." They said those fighters who hit the coast were only the advance troops of a larger army that remained in the interior.

According to Almada, the Mane attacked from two directions. A small group of "good sailors and swimmers" came from the **Malagueta Coast**. They must have lived there for a while to gain those skills. Among them were two Portuguese survivors of a shipwreck. Also with them was a Mandinka fighter previously employed in an attack on the Portuguese fort at Elmina. From

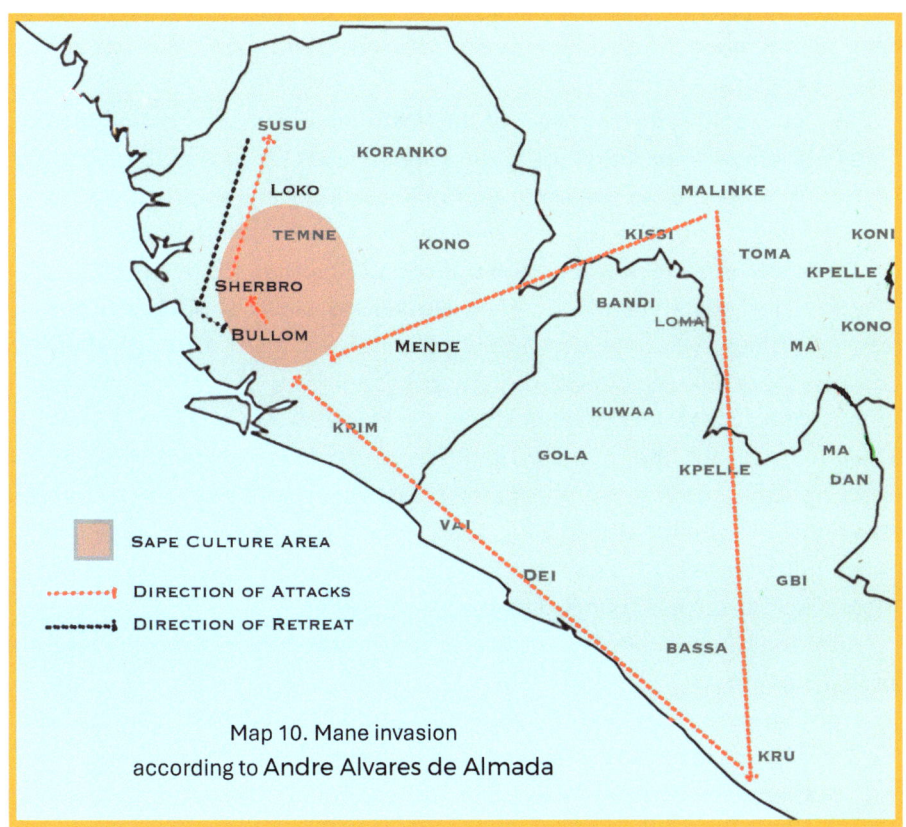

Map 10. Mane invasion according to Andre Alvares de Almada

the Gold Coast, he and other survivors apparently retreated to the Mandinka stronghold in the Konyan district. From there, they likely marched to seize key trading towns on the Malagueta Coast.

A much larger Mane army attacked from the interior. It was smaller when it started, but more fighters were recruited along the way. The Mandinka invaders apparently recruited members of ethnic groups on the border of present-day Guinea and Liberia. These included some Kissi, Mende and Bandi, who would all remain permanently in Sierra Leone. The invasion was reportedly planned by a general named **Mestre** who remained in the savannah with the rest of his army.

Robbing Graves and Eating Captives

According to Almada, the first Mane invaders came from the interior around 1560 CE and emerged in the region around **Sherbro Island**. They hit coastal communities hard. Their troops terrorized the local population in two ways. First, they **desecrated graves** as they searched for gold. Second, they cooked and ate some of their captives. Survivors fled, leaving empty town and villages.

Almada insisted that eating human flesh was not normal in any local culture. In fact, people were terrorized by **cannibalism** only because it violated deep seated taboos. But later racist scholars would cite such behaviors as normal among local people.

The Mane sold some prisoners to the **Portuguese**. Some who escaped fled onto Portuguese ships for refuge. Others were picked up by Portuguese sailors who went out patrolling the waterways in boats and small ships. All who landed in the hands of the Portuguese were carried away to a lifetime of slavery.

The first Mane attack was on the **Bullom**. During that battle, the defenders killed a Mane military leaders named **Masa Ricu**. News of his death quickly reached his homeland. He was probably from the maritime area of Malagueta Coast because a large number of fighters soon arrived by sea in a caravan of canoes, along with Ricu's wives and one of his sisters.

From the beach, they marched in military order to a chorus of drums. At the wake, his sister chose to mark her loss in a dramatic way. First, she rested the little finger of her left hand on a log. Next, she chopped it off with a large knife pulled from her belt. Ricu's sister then challenged his widows to do the same. Those who didn't were shunned by the Mane leaders.

After the burial, the Mane destroyed even more Bullom towns as revenge for Ricu's death.

From Sherbro Island, the invaders traveled 240 miles north-northwest to the Sierra Leone peninsula. They faced limited resistance from the various communities between Sherbro Island and the peninsula. They easily subjugated groups as they traversed hills, swamps and rivers. Next, they turned their attention to the Sape. Rather than fight against the invaders, the Sape ruler surrendered himself, his wives and many of his dependents to the Portuguese. Instead of being protected, they were taken into slavery.

Surrender or War

The Mane then shifted their focus to the **Soso**, a wealthy and powerful group in the region. Before the attack, the Mane followed their standard pattern. They sent their enemies an ultimatum in the form of cloths and arms. These items presented a stark choice: surrender or war. The Soso sent copies of their own weapons to indicate that they were prepared to fight.

This action offended the Mane who responded by collecting the largest set of weapons the region had ever seen. Their unusually large army included Portuguese **sharpshooters** and many of the people they had conquered. These details suggest the invasion was backed by wealthy funders.

Meanwhile, the Soso called on the **Fula** for help. The Soso army was led by men riding short Fula horses, decked with breastplates and great bells. They had archers in the center with **shield-bearers** in front and on either side. Both groups used short bows and poison arrows.

A Farewell Feast

As the Mane approached, the Soso sent a patrol ahead with several cows, which they killed and cooked in large pots. They left this food behind, making it appear that the Soso army had fled rather than fight the invaders. The hungry Mane soldiers devoured the food. Many quickly died because the food was poisoned.

The **Mane-Soso battle** lasted for days. But after 72 hours, the Mane fled across the river, pursued by the Soso and their allies. Only the fastest and bravest Mane soldiers were able to escape. The Soso killed or captured the rest. The Mane retreated to areas they had previously conquered, where they settled and ruled. But their aggression had plunged the whole area into chaos.

The ancestors of the Mende in Sierra Leone were apparently the core of the Mane army. They traveled about 200 miles from their earlier location around **Musadugu** in Guinea to settle around **Kenema** in Sierra Leone. Some settled among the Bullom, others among the Dama. Over time, the Dama language was replaced by Mende.

Overwhelmed by encroaching Mende and Kissi groups, the Gola moved from **Kongba**, their homeland, closer to the coast. They remembered the Malinke invasion as a time of hunger. There were too many people to feed and very little food. They believed the Mende, Loma, Kissi and Bandi had powerful "medicine" for warfare because those groups forced them from Kongba. The people known as Loko in Sierra Leone are descendants of Bandi who accompanied the Mane. They moved almost 200 miles from the area north of **Foya** in Liberia.

Writing 50 years after the Mane invasion, Almada said military conditions had changed. Local men had become better soldiers through regular drills.

Monkey Work, Baboon Draw

In the interior, the Mandinka seized grounds and changed the names of towns and even ethnic groups. Places like Kissidugu, Musudugu and Missadugu all include "***dugu***" which is the Malinké word for "town." The ancestral home of the Gola is often called "Kongba." But that name is not derived from their language. It is a Malinké word which means "**big bush**," which was given by the

Sketch of Fula fighters

Mane invaders. Worse still, the Mandinka referred to several local ethnic groups using curse words. **Belle** is what they called the Kuwaa, which means "savages," and labeled the Dan as **Gio**, meaning "slaves."

On the coast, the invaders' goal was likely not to seize and hold land. What they wanted was for local communities to work the land and pay taxes to their military overlords in the savannah. What they created was a system of tribute known as *marefe*. It is what Liberians call "monkey work, baboon draw."

Long before attacking Sherbro Island, one of the Mandinka "war houses" in southern Guinea had probably seized towns along the Malagueta Coast that were sites of significant trade with Europeans. They apparently imposed a similar **marefe** system on those towns. That would explain why fighters from the eastern coast of present-day Liberia aided the invasion of present-day Sierra Leone.

"Whites Did Not Sell Each Other"

After Europeans gained access to the Americas in the late 1400s CE, Spain abandoned its African trade in favor of **gold** mining and **sugar** production in what Europeans called "the New World." This shift led to a need for cheap labor. They turned to Africa because the capture and use of Native Americans proved unworkable.

Before the Mane invasion, Africans carried into slavery from this region had usually been kidnapped by Europeans directly or bought a few at a time from fellow Africans. But the Mane invasion set the stage for a dramatic change in scale. The previous Mandinka experience with the systematic capture and sale of Africans to the Middle East over centuries would now be applied to the Atlantic slave trade.

Between 1514 and 1562, at least 133 European ships carried African captives from between **Dakar** and **Cape Palmas**. Most of these vessels were from Portugal, the main foreign power then trading along the Guinea coast. Only three ships said they mainly bought slaves from Senegambia. The rest all listed **Cape Verde**. Africans bought there were brought from the mainland because those islands had very few residents.

But, in 1563 for the first time, three ships took captives from Sierra Leone. Those first captives from the area marked the start of a wave that lasted until 1568. During that time, seven more vessels carried 1,408 Africans away. One left there in 1564 and six vessels in 1568. Soon after the Mane invasion, they took between 537 and 1,127 captives to **slavery** in the Americas. All were taken to the Spanish-controlled island called **Hispaniola** and **Columbia** in South America.

One ship among the ten was Portuguese owned. Perhaps it was one of the Portuguese slave vessels mentioned by Almada. All the others were English owned. Other captives may have been taken to Cape Verde and resold to other places.

At first, the number of Africans taken from the **Windward Coast** to the Americas was low because the region did not have military capacity, population density or natural harbors. The dense forest along the Windward coast deterred slave traders from setting up major points of embarkation for the captives. The region's main initial role in the trans-Atlantic slave trade was to supply slave ships with water, firewood, salt, rice, yams and fowl. Going forward, large numbers of kidnapped people from present-day Liberia would be sold through **Gallinas**, **Sherbro Island** and **Freetown**.

Unlike other goods, the sale of kidnapped persons flowed in one direction only, as some Mane learned by a river one night. As beautiful flute music filled the air, they offered to buy the musician from the Portuguese. According to Almada, "Our men laughed at them, saying that this man was a white, and whites did not sell each other. They were not like blacks."

Civilians fleeing invaders

Quoja Invasion, 1620-1650 CE

After migrating from the area called **Burkina Faso**, ancestors of the Dan, Ma and Kru-language speakers settled on the northern edge of the forest belt.

Ma founded a town called **Karana**, from where all of their descendants dispersed. The Dan first settled in the **Gouane Mountain** near **Touba**. By 1620 CE, the Ma, Dan and Krahn lived near the town of **Man** in the mountainous savannah of northern Côte d'Ivoire. In those locations, they established trade links with Kru speakers who used these waterways to transport malagueta, kola, and salt.

According to oral traditions of the Ma and Dan, their ancestors knew how to forge iron weapons and cast **brass ornaments** before coming to Liberia. Metals are mentioned in the creation of stories of both groups. The Ma claim that after **Wala**, the creator, made the first family, **Nea Mia**, they descended from heaven on a chain. The Dan creation story tells of the first people descending from heaven in a brass basket.

Many ancestors of Ma, Dan, and Kru speakers faced pressures from Mandinka "war houses." They, too, migrated as some ancestors of the Kissi, Loma, Mende, Bandi and Kpelle had done. The Man and Dan traveled 130 miles from Man to Nzérékoré, before moving another 80 miles to Nimba in Liberia. Kru speakers walked over 200 miles from Man to **Grand Gedeh** in Liberia.

The Bassa claim Mt. Gedeh as their first home in the area. They consider the summit of the mountain to be the village of their dead. According to Bassa oral tradition, their ancestors were engaged in iron smelting and making iron tools while in Gedeh.

Most Kpelle ancestors lived in Missadougou, Guinea, one of their important and ancient towns. **Mouon**, a Kpelle resident of Musadugu, founded the town of **Guiéta**, which became the center of the Nzérékoré region. Guiéta was a point of transit used by many other groups migrating to Liberia.

Like their Loma neighbors to the west, religious strife erupted between the Kpelle and the Mandinka. A map of the Missadugu and Nzérékoré area in Guinea (page 102) shows the movement by Kpelle clans in red, Kono in purple and Dan in green. According to oral histories, those 10 clans moved due to Mandinka incursions.

The Kpelle say their ancestors made an agreement with Faran Kamara and his followers to respect local traditions. They gave vast farmlands in the area to him after his initiation into the Poro. Malinké oral traditions also acknowledge the existence of the "laws" in the Konyan region of Guinea that protected trading and traditional practices.

According to Kpelle oral history, they repelled the invading Mandinka of the Kouranko clan from Missadougou with help from the **Gou clan** of the Dan, who had settled among

For more information, see these:

Corker, Sylvester and Samuel Massaquoi, *Lofa County in Historical Perspective* (Monrovia: W. V. S. Tubman High School, 1972).

d'Azevedo, Warren L. *The Gola of Liberia* (New Haven, Conn.: Human Relations Area Files, 1972).

Dapper, Olfert. *Naukeurige Beschryvinghe der Afrikaensche gewesten* (Utrecht, 1668).

Davis, Ronald W. *Ethnohistorical Studies on the Kru Coast* (Newark, Del.: Liberians Studies Monograph Series No. 5, 1976).

Germain, Jacques. *Guinée: Peuples de la Forêt* (Paris: Académie des Sciences d'Outre-Mer, 1984).

Hair, P. E. H. "Barbot, Dapper, Davity: A Critique of Sources of Sierra Leone and Cape Mount," *History of Africa*. 1 (1974): 25-54.

Himmelheber, Hans. "Sculptors and sculptures of the Dan" (pp. 243-255), in L. J. Brown and M. Crowder, eds., *Proceedings of the First International Congress of Africanists* (Evanston: Northwestern University Press, 1964).

Korvah, Paul Degein. *The History of the Loma People* (Oakland, Ca.: O Books, 1995).

Riddell, James C.; Kjell Zetterström; Peter G. Dorliae; and Michael J. Hohl, "Clan and Chiefdom Maps for the Mā (Mano) and Dā (Gio)," *Liberian Studies Journal*, IV, 2 (1971-72): 157-162.

Schröder, Günter and Dieter Seibel, *The Liberian Kran and the Sapo* (Newark, Del.: Liberian Studies Association, 1974).

Siegmann, William. *Ethnographic Survey of Southern Liberia: Report on the Bassa* (Robertsport: Tubman Center of African Culture, 1969).

them. But, four Kpelle brothers and their followers later left Missadougou, fleeing attempts by the Mandinka to convert them to Islam. One brother named **Missa Coma Zoho** was a powerful **Poro Zoe**. Attracted by the lucrative coastal trade, he and his followers went southwest into Liberia. Those who moved to what is now Bong County travelled about 200 miles from their earlier location around Missadugu in Guinea.

Migrations from Man

During the 1600s CE, large numbers of well-armed Bambara and Mandinka from the north invaded northeastern Côte d'Ivoire. They converged near the headwaters of the **Sassandra** and **Bandama** rivers, especially on the trade towns of **Kong** and Man. Some Ma ancestors began moving west from the **Touba** region in the northwest Côte d'Ivoire towards Nzérékoré. According to Ma and Dan oral traditions, **women** led their migrations into Liberia.

Under pressure from the Malinke, the Ma people, who were migrating from Kong, met the Dan along the way. Those two groups journeyed together to the area of Nzérékoré, where they met the Kpelle and temporarily settled among them.

Some Dan migrated into the forest, where they settled among the Ma people in a town called *Guiepa* (in Mano) and *Guieta* (in Kpelle).

Oral traditions tell of two Ma brothers who stopped over in the town of Guiéta while traveling from the Touba region. One of them, **Mahou Yagbara**, used a gun to kill a leopard that had been troubling the area. As a reward, he was married to the local ruler's daughter and settled among the Kpelle.

Several secret societies existed among these groups, but only the Ma belonged to the Poro. While moving south, the Ma and Dan displaced some Kru-speakers, sending them into present-day Grand Gedeh County and down the **Cavalla River**.

Various Mande oral traditions also say their ancestors met Kru-speakers around **Sanniquelli**. Shared oral traditions of the Dei and **Settra Kru** say they previously lived close to Mande-speakers.

Many Kru-speakers living near the Ma and Dan formed long-term and close ties with them. Their wooden **masks** even shared a similar style. The most common mask had an idealized style of human figures showing no emotions. They featured elongated noses, slit mouths and geometrically shaped eyes. Some mask with frightening expressions were used for exorcism of evil forces.

Migrations from Mt. Gedeh

The Mandinka invaders dislodged many Kru-language speakers who had long lived near the Sassandra River. Among them were some ancestors of the Krahn, Kuwaa, Sapo, and Glebo. According to the oral traditions of several

Kru-speaking groups, their ancestors who came from Côte d'Ivoire migrated to Mt. Gedeh. The area was called **"Pahn"** because of the rich iron-ore deposits in the hills. One group migrated from **Njaja**, a town northeast of the Sassandra River. It included some ancestors of the Glebo, Klao, Kuwaa and Krahn.

When Krahn and Glebo ancestors entered into present-day Grand Gedeh County, their oral traditions claim they met a "fearful" people. As other groups converged atop Mt. Gedeh, the Bassa moved west. According to several oral histories, some of their ancestors settled around the town now called Musadugu. Others apparently traveled along the **St. John River** down to the coast.

Bassa Pushed South

Most Bassa later settled near the banks of the St. John and Junk rivers. While living on Mt. Gedeh, they had gained the skill of iron smelting. That enabled

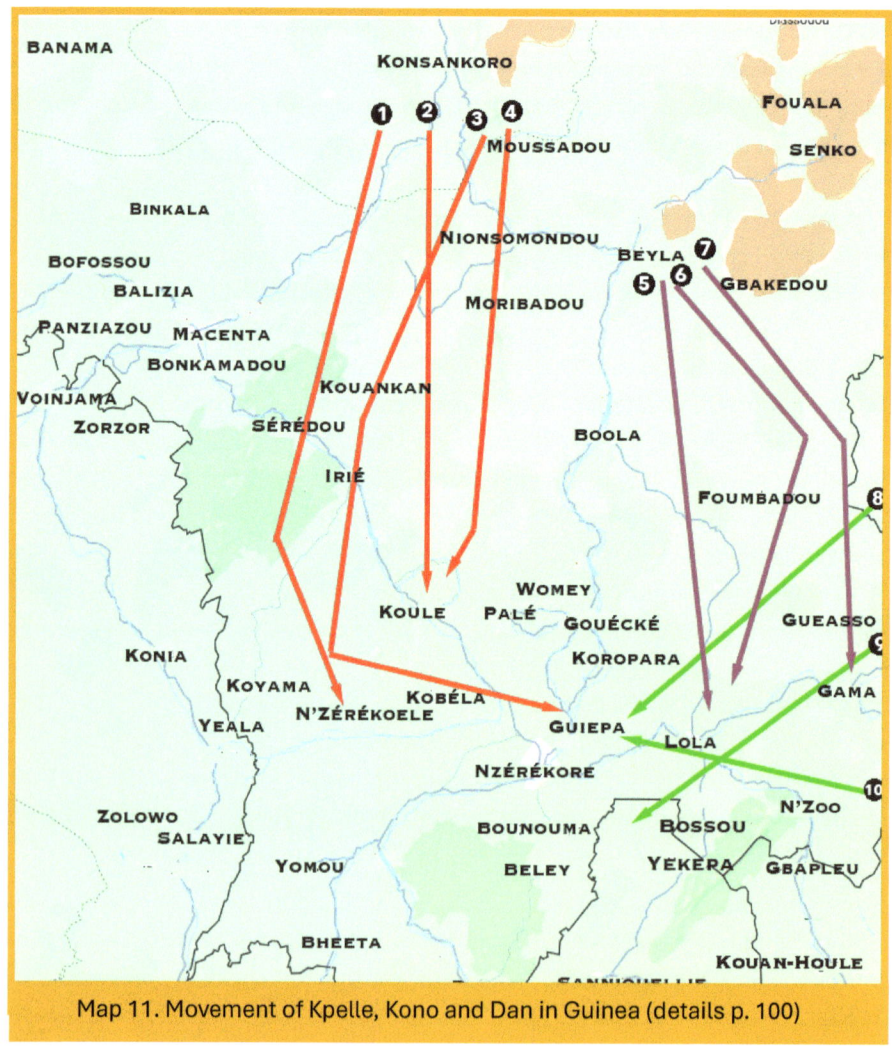

Map 11. Movement of Kpelle, Kono and Dan in Guinea (details p. 100)

them to smelt iron ore from **Mt. Finley**. Some went west toward the Montserrado River, where they met the Dei. The cape at the mouth of that river was home to many cats, so the Dei called it ***Blisue*** and the Bassa ***Sogila*** or ***Soila***; all three of these terms mean "cat hill."

Three signs suggest the Bassa are new to living by large bodies of water: First, their oral traditions say some of their ancestors met Europeans on the coast when they arrived. That means those ancestors reached the Atlantic shore after 1462 CE. Second, they credit the Klao with teaching them how to build canoes. Third, the Bassa have a unique set of folk tales devoted to fearful underwater creatures called Neegee, which their maritime Kru neighbors do not.

Glebo Migrate West

After living around Mt. Gedeh, many Kru-language speakers went west, like the Bassa and Kuwaa, or south, like the Klao. A Portuguese writer, who visited Cape Palmas in 1614, said the residents were called "***Gruvo***." Apparently, some Glebo were already living there. But some ancestors of the Glebo first went in a southeast direction to Grand-Bérébi in present-day Cote d'Ivoire.

The first Glebo settlements were **Nyomowe** (now Hoffman, west of Cape Palmas), and

A Dan power society mask

Red symbolized power, and sharp angles were associated with men. Cowrie shells were brought all the way from the East Africa. Because cowries were rare in West Africa, they were mysterious, exotic and once used as money.

Kudemowe (near Rocktown). Those two towns were the source of "fire" for all other Glebo settlements.

Klao Expansion

Early Kru-coast narratives often portray three culturally linked and mutually reliant groups. Each of them lived in separate places and engaged in different jobs.

The **Sapo**, an inland group, controlled trade with the interior. Based on their location, they were called "Bushmen" by some outsiders.

The other two groups lived on the Atlantic coast. As a result, they traded with Europeans and supplied young men to work on foreign ships. Those who fished were known as **Kle-po** or **Swa-po**, but English speakers called them "Fishmen." There were communities of "Fishmen" among the Bassa, Dei, and Vai. It was probably some of their ancestors in canoes who visited Pedro de Sintra's Portuguese fleet in 1462.

Those who farmed were called Krumen in English, but they called themselves **Nana-Kru**. Their ancestors had brought knowledge of rice farming with them when they migrated south from the forest edge. Originally, the Krumen inhabited the well-known *"Five Towns:"* Little Kroo, Setra Kroo, Kroo-Bar, Nana Kroo, and King Will's Town. But the "Kruman" label was later applied to most coastal Kru speakers, including the Glebo.

The Quoja Invasion

Between 1495 and 1505 CE, the **Kamara clan** had seized control of Nzérékoré district in present-day Guinea. After several generations in the savannah of present-day Guinea, they launched a major attack called the **Quoja**

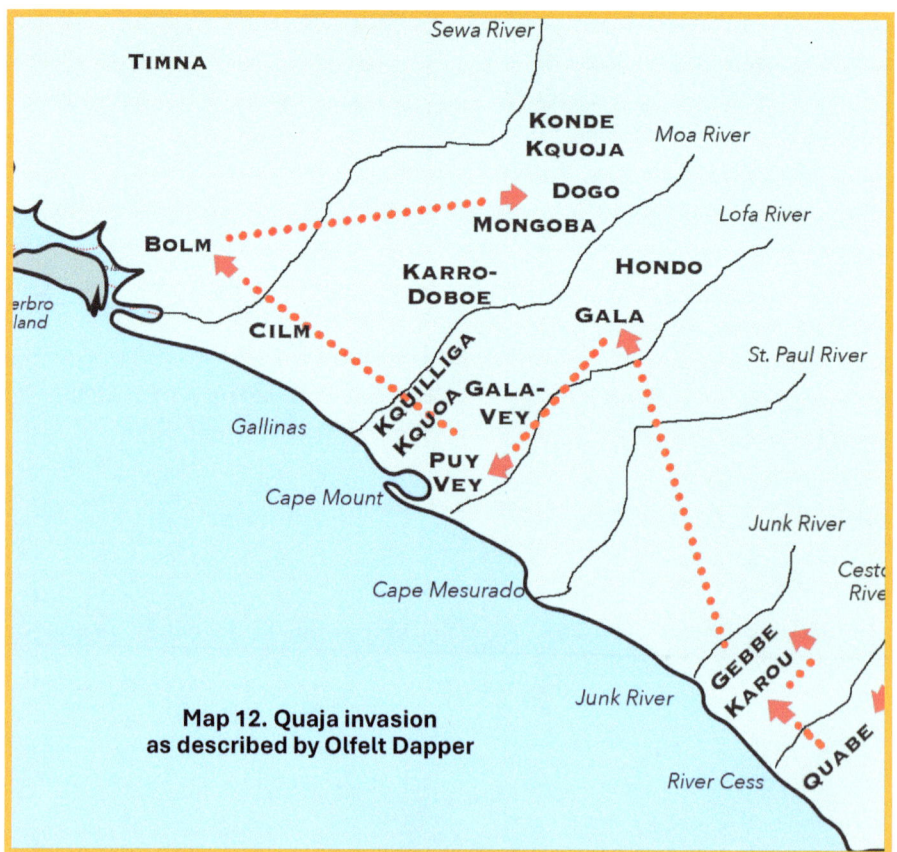

Map 12. Quaja invasion as described by Olfelt Dapper

invasion. They targeted coastal and forest communities in present-day Liberia between 1614 and 1651 CE.

Beginning near the edge of the **Nimba** Mountains, they apparently marched 158 miles south along the Cestos River. That route went through Kpelle and Bassa territories. They targeted the coast and interior from River Cestos to Sherbro Island. Their goal was to seize of the coastal trade with Europeans away from longtime residents. It disrupted life in the area now called Liberia far more than the Mane invasion.

Olfert Dapper, a Dutch geographer who never visited Africa, wrote an account of this invasion. He copied his account from a Dutch trader who lived in Cape Mount around 1626 CE. According to Dapper, Quoja leaders spoke "**Mendisco**," meaning **Mandingo**. But the army included recruits from diverse groups, including Kpelle fighters. The Kpelle and Ma together formed most residents in the Nzékékoré district, where the invasion began.

As some Kpelle, Ma, and Dan were pushed south, they displaced Kru speakers from the edge of the savannah into the forest. Many origin stories of Kru-speaking groups recount traveling toward the coast down parallel rivers. From Mt. Gedeh, some went along the St. John River before dividing. The oldest towns were near the headwaters of the rivers. Towns closer to the coast were called "junior" settlements.

Scene of Quoja country from book by Jean Barbot (see p. 114 for details).

The invaders conquered people in five places. Their victims along the coast included the **Gebbe** at the Junk River, the **Karou** at the St. John River, and the **Quabe** at River Cess. In the northwest interior of present-day Liberia, they subdued the **Gola** before moving south. At Cape Mount, their victims were the Vai and the nearby **Puy**. In Sierra Leone, they subdued the Bullom and **Dogo**. This invasion was one of the most disruptive in the region's history.

The **Folgia** sometimes provoked others to spark a fight. One feud began when the Folgia threw boiled fish with scales into a Karou pond. This act violated two of the group's well-known taboos. First, the pond was sacred to the Karou. It was the place where their first ancestor had descended "from heaven to earth." Second, they observed a strict prohibition against eating fish with scales. The enraged Karou went to war, but the Folgia defeated them.

Soon after that victory, the Folgia leader **Mendino** died. Suspicion fell on his brother, **Manimassah**, who then went through a trial-by-ordeal and survived. But he was offended, so he left the town where he was living. Manimassah then imposed himself as ruler of the Gola.

While traveling to Gola territory, Manimassah and his troops apparently met some Kru speakers. According to Krahn oral history, some of their ancestors were traveling with the Kuwaa along the northern border of present-day Liberia, but they divided when they met the Bassa. The Krahn retreated to Gedeh while the **Kuwaa** continued to the headwaters of the St. John River. They remained there until the Quoja invaders pushed them to what is now called **Gparpolu**.

After the Gola ousted him, Manimassah reimposed himself as their ruler, with help from his brother-in-law, **Flonikerry**, leader of the Folgia.

Gola Pushed South

After destabilizing Gola society, the Folgia launched a third unprovoked attack, this time on the Vai. According to Dapper, they were persuaded to do so by a man named **Fesiach**, who had previously lived among the Vai. His uncle, Flonikerry, had led the conquest of the Gola. Aided by the Karou, the Folgia warriors conquered the Vai, using bows and poison arrows.

Uprooted by the invaders, the Gola apparently began moving south over several generations. Some migrants created the towns of **Zoodi**, **Todien** and **Sugbulum** on the current Bomi Hill Road, as well as small remote villages between the Mano and St Paul Rivers. Some Gola groups went as far south as Cape Mount, where they joined the Vai and Dei. After leading many assaults, the Folgia began facing attacks from those they had subdued. The first to strike were the Gola led by Manimassa's son, Mininique. During the battle, the leading Folgia fighter, Flonikerry, was killed. But, with the help of the Vai, the Folgia were able to rally, defeat the Gola and subdue the Puy who lived close to the Vai.

Next to rebel were the Bullom and Dogo, two previously conquered groups. Folgia fighters returned to the Sherbro Island area and crushed the challengers. They then marched to the Junk River to subdue the rebellious Gebbe.

Thanks to Dapper, important information survived about the invasion. But he was apparently wrong about some details. For example, the leaders of the occupying force spoke the Quoja language, but not by the people they conquered. In addition, Dapper lumped together many types of groups that were different. Some were ethnic groups, like the well-known Gola and Vai. But Folgia was likely an army composed of fighters from different ethnic groups. The name probably came from **foroki**, a Malinké word meaning "to crush or grind."

The Dutch writer copied by Dapper probably relied on a Vai person for some of his information. That would explain why the writer called one group "**Monou**," which means "the people" in the Vai language. It is likely "the people" meant the leaders of the invasion, not an ethnic group. Dapper also makes the conflicts and fighting seem continuous. In reality, it likely occurred over many years.

Dapper's book leaves many gaps in the Quoja story. But he provides clues that help to fill in the blank spaces. For example, the leaders of various rival groups had Malinke names, like **Manimassa** and **Mendino**. This suggests many of the conflicts were family feuds. The desire to collect tribute motivated them, *not* ethnicity. In that case, Quoja leaders were warlords, not legitimate rulers. Their power derived more from fear than respect.

The Folgia often used fighters from among people they conquered to subdue other groups. For example, their leading fighter, **Flonikerry**, had a Kpelle-sounding name. That means combatants were probably paid mercenaries, who lacked ethnic or religious loyalty to Mandinka organizers of the invasion. The conflicts between the Mandinka and the people of the forest were not mainly ethnic. After all, clashes between empires and democratic societies are universal and timeless. Mali was like the **Roman Empire** centered in Italy. The smaller societies along the forest belt were similar to the city states of **Ancient Greece**. When face with a greater outside power, they either rallied together or faced certain defeat.

Because of the Mane and the Quoja invasions, the region now called Liberia was turned upside down for 100 years. Vast numbers of people living in the grasslands around major trade towns were forced from their ancestral homes into the forest. With their ironworking and other skills, they forged a new life in new lands. But those displacements scars the psyches of many survivors and their descendants.

British and **French** ships fighting in 1798 to seize control of the Nile River in Egypt. The two countries fought on the seas throughout the 1700s for control of foreign lands and global trade.

Shift in the Coastal Trade, 1650-1681 CE

Around 1650 CE, the northeastern region of present-day Côte d'Ivoire experienced another attack, this time from the east. Some Akan from a prosperous and populous empire in present-day Ghana poured across the Bandama River. They dislodged some ancestors of the **Eastern Krahn** and **Glebo** who fled to what is now called Liberia.

Glebo oral histories say some of their ancestors met a European slave barracoon on the coast when they arrived. That was likely sometime in the 1700s CE. Those Glebo ancestors were probably the ones carried from Cote d'Ivoire by canoes, not feet. Those who made it to Cape Palmas reportedly navigated the waves "like monkeys swinging through the trees." The name Glebo was derived from "*gle*-"for "monkey."

European trade along the West African coast led to a dramatic shift in the flow of African gold. By the 1500s, the Portuguese were exporting over half a ton of gold a year from the Gold Coast. The precious metal now went by sea directly to Lisbon, the capital of Portugal, instead of going overland by caravan to North Africa. This shift caused a slow decline in the economies of North Africa and the Sahel.

For 100 years, Portuguese kept the West African trade from other Europeans. They controlled the more profitable areas, like the Gold Coast, and built forts to block all trade rivals. They divided the overseas trade with Spain. The Portuguese kept to Africa while their Spanish cousins focused on the Americas. The two rivals often traded with each other through neutral Dutch merchants.

Overtime, the Dutch grew increasingly rich and powerful.

Until the 1500s CE, most of the European traders mainly remained along the coast. As a result, the writings of early European visitors offer only a glimpse of life in West Africa. Around 1533 CE, French, Dutch and English ship captains began arriving, but they kept to the less profitable stretches of the coast, like present-day Liberia. By 1600, the newcomers had driven the Portuguese from many trading posts. The written accounts of non-Portuguese traders included more details about the people and culture along the West African coast.

After 1554 CE, other European countries began seizing goods and territories previously held by the two major powers. Each nation sought a monopoly (meaning "total control") over importing textiles, spices and silver from Asia, precious metals and crops from the Americas, and gold and kidnapped workers from Africa.

That led to outbreaks of multiple wars in Europe. In addition, the ships of rival nations began fighting each other along the coast of West Africa, as they competed for control of foreign trade. But rivals did not use violence only against each other. Europeans used even more force against people in Asia, Africa and the Americas.

After 1621 CE, the Dutch made a concerted push into the Atlantic trade. From the Portuguese, they seized northeast **Brazil**, **Elmina** in western Africa, and **Luanda** in Angola.

For more information, see these:

Barbot, Jean. A Description of the Coast of North and South Guinea and of Ethiopia Inferior, Vol. 5, Book II, in Awnsham and John Churchill, **Collection of Voyages and Travels** (London: Awnsham and John Churchill, 1732).

d'Azevedo, Warren L. "Tribe and chiefdom on the Windward Coast," **Liberian Studies Journal**, Vol. 14, Issue 2 (1989): 90-116.

Dabien, G.; M. Delafosse; and G. Thilmans, "Barbot's Description of the African Coasts," **Bulletin de l'Institute francais d'Afrique noire**, Série B, 40 (1979): 235-395.

Dalby, David and P. E. H. Hair, "'Le langaige de Guynee': A sixteenth century vocabulary from the Pepper Coast," **African Language Studies**, 5 (1964).

Green, John. **A New General Collection of Voyages and Travels**, Vol. 2 (London: Thomas Astley, 1745-47).

Hair, P. E. H. "An early seventeenth-century vocabulary of Vai," **African Studies**, 23, 3-4 (1964): 129-139.

Hair, P. E. H. "Some French sources on Upper Guinea, 1540-1575," **Bulletin de l'Institute francais d'Afrique noire**, Série B, t, 31, no. 4 (1969): 1030-1034.

Hair, P. E.; Adam Jones; and Robin Law, eds., **Barbot on Guinea: The Writings of Jean Barbot on West Africa 1678-1712** (London: The Hakluyt Society, 1992).

Sundstrom, Lars. **The Exchange Economy of Pre-Colonial Tropical Africa** (New York: St. Martin's Press, 1974).

Swanzy, F. "A French voyage to West Africa in 1666-1667," **Journal of the Royal African Society**, Vol. 7, No. 26 (Jan. 1908): 190-204.

Villault, Sieur de Bellefond Nicolas. **A Relation of the Coasts of Africk called Guinee** (London: John Starkey, 1670).

A French Ship Called Europa

Between 1666 CE and 1667 CE, the French West Indian Company sent a ship called the *Europa* to West Africa to investigate trading options secretly. The mission was led by **Nicolas Villault de Bellefond**, who left a detailed account of his trip.

On January 8, 1666, the ***Europa*** anchored off the coast of Cape Mount. Villault and some of his crew rowed to shore in small boats. They came across five huts, where people were boiling seawater to make salt. The salt makers sent word that foreigners had arrived to their ruler, who lived three days away.

The next morning the ship's crew fired two guns to let the local people know they wanted to trade. In response, the villagers lit fires onshore as a signal that they had goods to trade. The ship crew spent the next two days buying local goods, mainly ivory.

After four days, Villault returned to the shore. Rough waves prevented his small boat from landing. As a result, he was carried part of the way on the backs of crew members. On shore, he found that the residents had built a large thatch-covered marketplace to keep the trade goods dry and to shelter traders from the hot sun. News spread fast about the French trader. People soon came from far and wide, constructed temporary shelters, and filled them with goods for trading.

Arrival of the Ruler

After trading started, Villault saw people running from their homes and temporary shelters; some even abandoned their trade goods. They were running to welcome their ruler, Falam Boure, and his entourage.

Falam Boure wore a blue robe. The men of his entourage were dressed in blue-and-white striped gowns, made from woven cotton that Liberians call "country cloth." Villault described the ruler as grave, venerable, sensible, majestic and probably over 60 years old. Speaking in Portuguese, Falam Boure told his guests that it had been four years since any whites had visited Cape Mount.

According to Villault, a person's social status was defined locally by their clothes and their dwellings. The houses of the rich and powerful were divided into distinct rooms with one of the rooms for night-time sleeping. This room contained an elevated plank or mat bed that was screened off by a cloth. For day-time rests and naps, rich people reclined on delicate mats.

Millet, Maize and More

Villault noted that rice, millet, and maize were plentiful. They grew here in greater quantities than any other part of the coast, he said. The fruits he identified were citrons, oranges, melons, gourds and a sort of plum. He bought a variety of fowls at cheap prices. These included hens, pigeons, and ducks. Other sources of meat were tortoises, goats, pigs, and apes. Fish were also plentiful from both the sea and rivers. Over the course of four days, the *Europa* crew bought mainly mats, rice, and ivory. Villault was impressed by the scenic beauty of the land and rivers, the humor and disposition of the people, the wealth made from trade, and the design of the buildings. On January 13, the *Europa* sailed away.

A Ruler Robed in Red

Villault arrived at Cape Mesurado after a day of sailing. The coast was covered by a thick fog. The crew fired two guns to let the local people know they were interested in trading. The next day, two local men in a canoe approached and boarded the ship. They told Villault it had been a year since the last white trader had visited. His visitors promised they would bring him a lot of ivory the next day.

But Villault was worried about being at Cape Mesurado. He had heard terrible stories about both its people and the nearby waters. The next day, Villault and his crew went ashore heavily armed. The local people were quick to notice his fear. They asked him why he brought a canon with him if he wanted to trade in peace. Villault made his way to the village where he found the local ruler, along with 60 of his entourage, sitting under a tree armed with darts, bows, arrows and swords. Upon his arrival, the few women present immediately retreated to the woods.

African ivory porters

The ruler was dressed in a red robe with a red hat. Villault described him as a forceful and severe man. Presented with two bottles of brandy, he and his companions quickly consumed them. After this, trading began. At Cape Mesurado, trading centered on ivory and rice, both of which were plentiful.

Villault's visit was short. But he quickly learned that the local people had great respect for their priests and ancestors. He also claimed that the local people believed in the power of their **ritual objects**, which he dismissed as "fetishes," meaning "false gods." During dinner, the leading men honored offered a libation of palm wine to their ancestors.

Although Villault saw good quality ivory, he felt the price was too high. Without buying any tusks, he sailed the next day for River Cess.

Shaking Hands and Snapping Fingers

Near River Cess, local fishermen approached the ship and told Villault there was plenty of ivory. Accompanied by some of his crew, he canoed nine miles up the river. At a village there, he presented the ruler of the area with gifts. Villault described him as a forceful, stern and haughty person. According to Villault, the Malaguetta Coast ran for 150 miles from Sanguin River to Cape Palmas. He listed the names of several towns along this stretch of the coast as *Cestros-Crou, Brova, Battou, Sino, Crou Sestre, Wappo, Botou, Grand Sester, Petit Sester,* and *Goiane*. Each town was located on the bank of a river, the main ones being the Sanguin and Grand Sestra.

People along the Malaguetta Coast had a unique way of greeting each other, Villault said. The salutation consisted of grasping each other by the upper arm while saying "**Toma**." They then said "*Toma*" again while clasping the elbow hard. They ended by snapping fingers and saying "*Enfa Nemate*," which meant, "All that I have is at your service."

Villault thought the land around **River Cess** was fertile. The area had a good supply of fowl, rice and millet. Although there was a large quantity of ivory, he felt the price was too high. Again, he left empty-handed.

The ship sailed for the Sanguin River. While the frigate was anchored, the local ruler came aboard. Like his Cape Mount counterpart, the ruler at Grand Cess wore a blue cotton robe. Villault described him as a very grave, serious, and large man with white hair. Although elderly, he was still vigorous. During the visit, the ruler surprised Villault by not drinking wine, strong alcoholic drink or even palm wine. The ruler's brother also visited the ship. He spoke fluent **Dutch**, having spent three years in Holland. Villault learned that a small ship with a mainly Dutch crew had recently kidnapped about 12 people from Crou Sester.

The French man did not go ashore, but he guessed the town had about 100 huts. He learned the area had a large supply of rice and millet. It produced beans, citrons, oranges, peas, plums and nuts. There was also a good supply of cows, goats, hogs, chicken and other fowl. In addition, there was good **palm wine**.

At Grand Cess, the ship's shears were mended. These scissors were used to cut iron bars. The crew was very impressed with the work of the local **blacksmiths**. They not only sharpened the shears but made them stronger. According to Villault, the repair made the scissors better than when they were *new*.

Villault's record of his travels showed that ship traffic along the Malaguetta Coast was frequent. But vessels from different European nations often attacked each other. The *Europa* even attempted to capture a similar-sized ship, but backed off as the other ship had more firepower.

Beautiful Canoes

A Frenchman named **Jean Barbot** published one of the first detailed books in English about the area of present-day Liberia. Born in France, he served as a commercial agent on French slave-trading ships to West Africa in 1679-1680 and again in 1681. After returning home, he wrote about his visits to the Guinea Coast in 1683.

But Barbot fled to England two years later to escape religious persecution. Originally written in French, his book was translated to English and published in 1732, after his death.

Barbot left first-hand observations of River Cess. He spent eight days on land, but slept onboard his ship at night.

Barbot included many detailed descriptions and drawings of the area that no one had recorded before. One sketch (p. 105) featured a porcupine, a jackal and a leopard (walking into a trap) at the front. In the middle is an egret. In the back, people seem to be farming, burning wood and carrying someone in a hammock.

Barbot praised residents of the Malagueta Coast for their rice and millet framing. He said they also decorated their canoes beautifully. He said, "The Dutch used formerly to export a great quantity of malagueta yearly, loading whole ships; but it is now less sought after."

A Long List of Villages

Barbot recorded a long list of village names along the Malagueta Coast and the distances between them. From west to east, they were: River Cess to Little Sestros (14-and-a-half miles), Little Sestros to **Cap das Baixos Svino** (one-and-a-half miles), Sanguin to **Baffa** (four-and-a-half miles), and Baffa to Serres (six miles). From Serres to **Crou Setter** was 15 miles. Between them were Dassa, **Buttouwa**, **Sabrebou** and **Sinou**. From Crou Sestro to Wappo was 15 miles. Be-

Jean Barbot meeting with the ruler of River Cess (see p. 116 for details)

tween them were **Badoe**, **Droe** and **Niffa**. From Droe to Grand Cess was ten-and-a-half miles.

From the sea, several features of some towns were visible:

- Cape des Baixos had several small rocks to the south and one big one with a tree to the north.
- Bottouwa sat on a large cliff.
- Wappo stood near a large island and three rocks in the sea. Bird droppings covered one rock, which made it look white. Barbot did not land at Wappo, but, he thought it looked as large as **Elmina**, a Gold Coast town.
- Cape Palmas was shaded by palm trees on all sides. That is how the place got its name.

People living between Bottouwa and Wappo carried goods in baskets shaped like a tall cone with a rounded top. At Grand Cess, some residents spoke **French**.

From the St. John River to Cape Palmas, people swore **oaths** in a similar way. They would take sea water and put a handful on their head three times, as a promise "not to cheat." Unlike people in other towns, the residents of Little Sestro and Cap das Baisox Svino specialized in fishing.

Barbot spent most of his time at River Cess. He traveled at least six miles up the river. The local villages ranged from 25 to 150 huts. Houses were built on pillars, with their floors three-and-a-half feet above the ground. People climbed a ladder to enter. This elevated design probably protected residents from predatory animals like **leopards**. Some interior walls were printed black or red.

A clay wall about six feet high surrounded one inland village. As kidnappings for the slave trade increased, more and more villages would later build surrounding walls to protect their residents.

But one building stood outside the village wall. It was circular and 60-feet wide, with a pointed roof. This was a palava hut where officials received visitors. Barbot called it "the Whiteman's Hut." A wooden statue of a woman and child stood at the center. People came before the **icon** to swear oaths and place offerings of food and drink.

First Mention of Barsaw

Barbot was the first writer to mention words that sounded like "Bassa" in reference to the area near River Cess. He referred to the ruler of the region as a man named **Barsaw**, who was also called "**Pieter**." His territory covered 105 miles from the St. John River in the west to Crou Setter in the east. Several other European visitors to River Cess in 1693, 1701 and 1727 cited a ruler there named Peter, Pieter, or Pedro.

During Barbot's visit, Barsaw lived in an inland village. The French visitor described his host as dressed in a white gown with embroidery of various colors. He sat hunched on his heels, smoking a pipe with the bowl resting on the ground. In front of him were two large pots of palm wine.

One sketch from Barbot's book shows his meeting with Barsaw (p. 114). It includes capital letters next to certain figures: A. The King of Sestro; B. The King Councellours; C. My Self; D. My assistants; E. My presents to the King; F. The King's Presents; G. The Idol of the King; and H. The Hearth. Barbot's dash of two iron bars and two flasks of brandy are visible in the drawing. In the lower right corner of the engraving are Barsaw's presents of a large basket of rice and two hens. Visible on the floors in the engraving are two long iron bars, two flasks of brandy, a sheaf of rice and two hens.

Early Days of "Dash"

Barbot described Barsaw's hair as **braided** to two points on the side, like animal horns. His straw hat was shaped like a cone and decorated with small **porcupine tails** and other items. A necklace with two young-goat **horns** hung near his stomach. According to the Way of the Ancestors' teachings, horns and tails were energized with life-force. Barsaw's assistant, **Jacob**, was a priest and doctor who knew the healing properties of plants. He lived in a village on the coast.

Along the West African coast, people usually exchanged gifts before doing business. Barbot **dashed** Barsaw two iron bars, a bundle of glass beads, two flasks of **brandy** and a few knives. In return, he received a large basket of rice and two hens.

Barsaw reportedly had 30 wives, but his visitor only saw six. According to Barbot, men at River Cess married as many women as they could maintain. At mealtime, the father ate first, then the mother, followed by the children.

According to Barbot, women dressed simply, with a cloth tied "round their loin." Mothers carried babies in "a kind of leather box" tied to their backs "to prevent accidents." In his opinion, mothers here were "out-

This Bassa sculpture shows **raised tatoos** on the chest and forehead.

standing in their **tender care** for their infants." Barsaw's head wife's body was decorated with **raised tattoos**, like many women in the region. Hers were confined to her arms, legs, and middle, but others were covered from head to feet. To get those raised tattoos, people applied hot irons to their skin.

The other "Bassa" sounding word recorded by Barbot was the name of a river called "Little Barsay." It divided the "**Quabee**" people of Sestros to the east, from the "**Monou**" people to the west. Those group names echo two warring factions linked to the earlier Quoja invasion. In Dapper's text from 1670, he placed the Manou and Quabe on opposite banks of the Scarcies River in Sierra Leone. But Dapper never visited the region. For that reason, his geographical claim is less trustworthy than Barbot's.

Mandinka Presence at River Cess?

Barbot's book also hints at a Malinké cultural presence at River Cess two or three decades after the Quoja invasion. The local ruler, he said, was seated in a palava hut with about 20 prominent men dressed like Moors or Arabs. They wore little bells around their arms, legs, shoulders and waists, as well as glass beads of various colors. A few wore iron rings on their legs that weighed over 3 lbs. In common with Arabs and Moors, men were circumcised. They wore their hair platted like men at Cape Mount.

Shrines and Sacrifices

Barbot included many comments on the supply and uses of local foods. There were beans, plenty of kola, some pineapples, bananas, oranges, lemons and many yams. From boiled yams, residents made a "pap" that they fed to their children.

Rice bird nest from book by Jean Barbot

The staple food was boiled rice. People rolled it into balls in their hands. They ate it with mutton, fish, chicken, goat, and monkey meat, which was a favorite. Chickens were so cheap that Barbot bought several for trinkets worth a penny.

Barbot visited River Cess during the rice-planting season, which was often a time of food shortages. But he was still able to buy 600 lbs. of rice and 200 chickens. He compared the quality of both to those of Lebanon. He said the local rice was not as large or as white. But the local chickens tasted better.

Barbot was the first visitor to record descriptions of two rituals related to the Way of the Ancestors along the coast of present-day Liberia.

One was a shrine with rocks around it outside the village. It contained a two-foot-high image of a man made from dark brown soil. Every evening, Barbot saw Barsaw and others wash themselves before visiting the shelter to offer chickens as sacrifices. The other ritual involved dancing and offering sacrifices to ensure a good harvest. It was performed one day before rice planting. Many people took part, including visitors from outlying areas. Some smeared their faces with blood, which was then covered with flour.

"Much Human Feeling"

Barbot described River Cess residents as having "much human feeling." He recalled a night when a **storm** forced him and about 34 crew members to shelter on land at 10 pm. It was "delightful to see these good people come from all sides," he said. Some brought salt, others rice, wood, and water. They repeatedly hugged a young Wolof boy from Senegambia, who came ashore with Barbot's crew. At one point, 40 of his men fell ill from working on shore. Several of them took a long time to recover. Their symptoms included violent headaches, vomiting, pains in the bones, terrible fevers, and confused brains.

The illness sounds a lot like malaria. But in the late 1600s CE, people did not know it was spread by mosquitos. Barbot thought the air rising from swampy ground caused the disease. So, he decided to keep his crew aboard the ship at night, especially during the rainy season.

1,000 Bird Nests in One Tree

Barbot described some animals he saw, and he even drew pictures of a few. In his words, some caterpillars were "hideous." The sting of large green flies could draw blood. The bite of large ants in the woods caused "painful blisters." To him, the dogs were ugly. The sheep were similar in size to those in Europe but without wool.

The local **birds** impressed Barbot with their brilliant colors and skills. He said one tree on the coast was filled with 1,000 nests of weaver birds. According to him, the nests were so strong and well built, they sheltered the birds in any weather. He admired the artistic work of those "feeble creatures."

Sugar and Slavery

After 1637 CE, sugar **plantations** rapidly increased in the Caribbean. That led to a demand for more kidnapped Africans. England and other European countries joined the race to buy African captives too. Most Windward captives went to the sugar plantations of the Caribbean, including Antigua, 11,857; St. Kitts, 8,301; Domiinica, 10,749; Barbados, 15,121; Grenada, 14,423; Jamaica, 32,863; and Saint-Domingue, present-day Haiti and Dominican Republic, 8,055.

Sugar production was labor intensive. Enslaved people planted the crops and kept rats from eating the growing canes. At harvest time, they worked in groups to cut the ripe cane, strip the outer leaves and tie the stalks into bundles. After juicing the cane, they boiled it to produce sugar and molasses. These jobs were backbreaking and dangerous. Many enslaved Africans died or lost limbs during the boiling of sugar.

In the late 1690s CE, Europeans rushed to remove gold from Brazil, a country in South America. which dramatically boosted the demand for labor. At first, mine operators forced Native Americans to remove gold and silver. This proved unsuccessful, as many of them fled into the jungles or died from abuse and disease.

To replace them, Europeans greatly increased the number of captives brought from Africa. They believed Africans had better resistance to tropical heat and diseases. All European naval powers were soon scrambling for lands in the Americas and for enslaved Africans to work those lands. But some Africans soon fled in the rainforests of Brazil too.

Gola and Kissi Become Gullah and Geechee

Operators of the trans-Atlantic slave trade decided to grow **rice** in the Americas instead of buying it in Africa to feed captives on **slave ships**. To do that, they decided to import rice seeds and African captives who knew how to grow rice.

As early as 1685 CE, **South Carolina** and **Georgia** in the U.S. and Surinam (formerly Dutch Guiana) in South America became rice-growing areas using people, knowledge, and seeds from West Africa. Buyers of African captives requested their local allies to capture rice-growing people from the Windward Coast. As a result, 12,610 Windward captives were taken to the rice-growing swamps of South Carolina and Georgia, with only 3,406 carried to other parts of North America. Some were ancestors of the Kissi and Gola who became known as **Geechee** and **Gullah**.

By 1669 CE, the Dutch had more ships than all other European countries combined. They also had greatly increased the trade in African captives. As the Dutch tightened their control of world trade, their presence increased in the area now known as Liberia. While the Dutch were challenging the Portuguese and Spanish, the English and the French used the opportunity to seize territories in the Americas.

After a 90-year lull, the selling of Africans to Europeans spiked between Cape Mesurado and present-day Cote d'Ivoire. Between 1654 and 1664, six ships removed 1,254 captives. For the first time, vessels listed the Sassandra River and Cape Mount as places where slaves were bought. All the others were taken from Sierra Leone. Two of the ships were Dutch, two English, one French and one Spanish. They took the Africans to **Curacao**, the **Canary Island** and **Barbados**.

African captives being lowered into the hold of a slave ship.

Slavery, Scarcity and Suspicions, 1700-1800 CE

In the mid-1700s, a third incursion occurred in the savannah. This time the town called Man in present-day Cote d'Ivoire was besieged by invaders from the collapsed Songhai Empire. They displaced the **Northern Krahn** toward Mt. Gedeh. According to Krahn oral traditions, those ancestors moved to escape the attackers and in search of wild game.

Along the Windward Coast, **Britain** and **France** were competing to replace the Dutch as the dominant power. They repeatedly fought each other on both sides of the Atlantic over land, furs, precious metals, cash crops, and African captives. In the 1600s CE, European countries created 28 colonies in the Americas. The Dutch had three, France eight and England 17.

Between 1763 and 1783, Britain emerged as the dominant world power. Its rise was fueled by the exploitation of both India and colonies in the Americas, worked by enslaved Africans. The number of English people living in the Caribbean islands was double that of any other European nation. In North America, the French colonies of **Quebec** and **Louisiana** were small compared to England's North America colony. After losing territories to England in during the late 1700s, the French turned increasingly to Africa.

The rivalry between the Dutch, English and French were evident on the Windward Coast.

From 1686 to 1702 CE, a Dutch merchant named Willem Bosman spent 16 years in West Africa. He served as the Dutch East India Company's chief agent, mainly at Fort Elmina on the Gold Coast. During his time there, he wrote 22 letters to his uncle in Holland describing life in West Africa. From Nov. 28 to Dec. 25, 1701 CE, he visited Cape Mount, Cape Mesurado, Corra, River Cess, and Settre Crou. In 1704 CE, his letters were published in a book.

Many Elephants, But Few Tusks

On Nov. 28, 1701, Bosman stopped at Cape Mount, hoping to buy ivory. He saw three villages on the coast with about 30 huts. After he landed, people quickly filled the shore. **Lake Piso**, he noted, overflowed into the Atlantic Ocean once a year, during the rainy season.

After one hour, the ruler of Cape Mount arrived with an entourage. Jan, as he was called, wore a brown cloak and an imported woolen cap. Bosman described him as an old man with grey hair. Jan reportedly had 400 wives who lived in the same village with him. The Dutch visitor was told each man was allowed as many wives as he could maintain.

Bosman described Cape Mount residents as hard working. Their primary jobs were growing rice and making sea salt.

The many leopards and elephants in the area often disrupted community life. Lake Piso was filled with fish, which people caught using large nets. Pineapples and bananas were available, but staples were scarce, especially yams and potatoes.

For more information, see these:

Alpern, Stanley B. "What Africans got for their slaves: A master list of European trade goods, **History in Africa**, Vol. 22 (1995).

Bean, Richard. "A note on the relative importance of slaves and gold in West African exports," **Journal of African History**, XV, 3 (1974): 351-356.

Curtin, Phillip D. **The Atlantic Slave Trade: A Census** (Madison: University of Wisconsin, 1969).

Gemery, Henry A. and Jan S. Hogendorn, "The economic costs of West African participation in the Atlantic slave trade: A preliminary sampling for the Eighteenth Century," in Henry Gemery and Jan Hogendorn, **The Uncommon Market** (New York: Academic Press, 1979).

http://www.slavevoyages.org/tast/index.faces.

Inikori, J. E. **Forced Migration: The Impact of the Export Slave Trade on African Societies** (New York: Africana Publishing Co., 1982).

James, C. L. R. T**he Black Jacobins** (New York: Vintage, 1963).

Jones, Adam and Marion Johnson, "Slaves from the Windward Coast," **Journal of African History** 21 (1980): 17-34.

Rediker, Marcus. **The Slave Ship: A Human History** (New York: Viking, 2007).

Smith, Frederick H. **Caribbean Rum: A Social and Economic History** (Gainesville: University Press of Florida, 2005).

Terborg-Penn, Rosalyn. "Women and slavery in the African diaspora: A Cross-cultural approach to historical analysis," **Sage**, Vol. III, No. 2 (Fall 1986),

Bosman left Cape Mount after finding only two tusks to buy. Foreign demand for ivory during this period nearly wiped out West African elephants. Bosman arrived at Cape Mesurado on Nov. 29, but no residents approached his ship.

Mesurado Ravaged by English Men

According to the Dutch man, two large **English ships** had attacked several Mesurado villages two months earlier. They ravaged the area, destroyed all the canoes, plundered houses, and captured some people who were carried into slavery. Survivors fled inland, and most of them were still there. Residents were determined to seize an equal number of English men, if possible.

Bosman saw three villages with 20 houses on Bushrod Island. Each house had three apartments, with about 20 people in each. He said the houses were the finest he had seen on his voyage. Their tops were covered "like our **Hayreaks** in Holland."

Along the West African coast, visitors were expected to give their host a present, called a *dash* in Portuguese. The Dutch visitor dashed two local leaders with seven pounds of **copper**. He said most local men were traders, while the women did most of the other chores.

There was plenty of excellent palm wine, pineapples, bananas, yams, and potatoes. A traffic of canoes went daily to River Cess and back. Bosman bought 300 lbs of ivory before sailing toward River Cess. Along the way, he only saw a few villages that seemed occupied by people making sea salt.

Three miles from River Cess, local people in a canoe came aboard his ship. They lured him to land based on a promise of ivory. Their town called **Corra** was not on any European map. After walking a quarter mile, he was disappointed to discover two salt-boiling villages. One had 12 houses, the other had six. He thought the residents had never seen a white person before.

It seems the people had recently moved from the interior to the coast. They were possibly those Bassa ancestors who, according to oral tradition, met Europeans on the coast when they arrived.

Bosman thought the residents looked "wild and strange." But they were "very civil and courteous." One resident was a mother with quadruplets. An old man, who looked like their leader, insisted that Bosman eat and drink before returning to his ship. Finding no ivory available, Bosman left, disappointed.

Multistory Houses "Neatly Built"

On Dec. 3, Bosman reached River Cess. He was impressed by the landscape. There were two high hills; one looked like a semicircle. To the east, a **peninsula** extended into the ocean. But the river mouth was filled with rocks, hidden six-feet below the surface.

Villages lined the river bank. One village had houses "**very neatly built**" with several stories. They were so high, people on ships at sea could see them from three miles away. Bosman praised local people for being "very industrious." He said growing rice was their major job. According to him, there was enough rice to fill a ship.

The ruler of the area lived three miles up the river. His name was **Peter**, like many rulers on the Windward Coast. The Dutch visitor described him as a very old man with gray hair. He was "very agreeable" and "obliging."

According to Bosman, the residents of Peter's village were all his descendants. But this might have been a mistranslation since the words used for "papa" and "clan leader" were similar in several local language. Instead, the residents may simply have been the ruler's *dependents*.

Bosman asked if there were any wars in the area, as he had earlier asked at other places. He apparently was trying to learn if captives were available to buy. Residents told him people from the interior had recently burned a local village in a surprise attack. Locals retaliated, seized many of the inland attackers and sold them into slavery.

A Local Funeral and Wake

Bosman recorded one significant **rite of passage** – a funeral for an old woman. His account was probably the first written description of a local death ceremony. According to him, the woman's body was immediately covered with a cloth and surrounded by villagers. Young and old brought **banana leaves** to shield the corpse from the sun. Men started howling and rushing from the

Cape Mesurado village from book by Chevalier des Marchais (p. 128 for details)

woman's house. Women began crying loudly. The mourning continued for about 24 hours. A day later, the body was placed in a canoe with one pot of rice, another of palm wine, and a variety of greens.

Ten young "vigorous" men carried the loaded canoe to the river. The body was taken for burial to the birthplace of the deceased. Relatives and friends returned from the burial three days later. They brought a sheep and a good supply of palm wine for a feast. Bosman joined them in eating and drinking "heartedly," not knowing that he was expected to help pay for the feast.

According to Bosman, local traders were constantly involved in selling rice, malagueta, and some ivory. But fear prevented him from exploring River Cess fully: English ships were prowling the ocean nearby, and the Dutch regarded them as enemies.

Boman sailed east from River Cess on Dec. 11, after eight days of trading. Little Sestre laid three miles away. Next to it was a mountainous rock with a very high tree. Sanguin was a mile-and-a-half further. From there, a large, white-colored rock jutted into the ocean. It looked like a ship sail when seen from the sea. According to Bosman, Sanguin residents liked taking goods without paying for them.

An English-Speaking Ruler Named James

Bosman next stopped at Bossoe, a mile further east. A local ruler named James came aboard. He spoke a mixture of English and Portuguese.

Bosman next stopped at Bottawa, about three miles away. Two large rocks in the sea framed it. One was half a mile to the west, the other a mile to the east. Residents brought malagueta to the ship, which he bought.

A mile-and-a-half away was Sino. He dismissed the local language as "barbarous" because he couldn't understand it.

On Dec. 20, Bosman reached Settre Crou. It laid on lowland and had two large rocks on the shore. He described the village as "**beautiful**" and larger than Elmina on the Gold Coast. The town was well furnished with cattle and fruits similar to Cape Mount. The fish reminded him of those on the Gold Coast.

Bosman described the local people as good and honest. But he dismissed their language as "utterly unintelligible."

After trading, Bosman sailed three miles east to Wappo. He described it as marked by a large rock on the shore and a high red-colored hill. From Wappo, the land was flat for three miles. At Cape Palmas, a point of land jutted into the sea. From a distance, it looked like a dolphin. He saw no villages or people at Cape Palmas, so he sailed away on Christmas night.

On Dec. 9, 1724, **Chevalier des Marchais**, a French spy, cartographer and slave-ship captain, visited the Windward Coast. He left one of the most detailed accounts of the people and geography of Cape Mesurado. Marchais noted two islands in the Mesurado bay. The bigger one is now called Bushrod Island. The smaller one was known for a time as **Gomez Island**.

A Constant Sea Breeze, But No Fresh Water

According to Marchais, Bushrod was called the ruler's island, although he lived elsewhere. Some of his people there raised cattle and poultry for his use. The island was cool because of a constant sea breeze that was not obstructed. But it lacked fresh water, which had to be brought from springs on the mainland.

Marchais' book included a sketch of a Cape Mesurado village (p. 126). It shows a palava hut on left and kitchen on the right. Most buildings are elevated as protection from flooding or predatory animals.

The local ruler in 1726 was called **Captain Peter**, a name which was commonly used by generations of **tawu** or rulers of Mesurado.

According to Marchais, *Tawu* Peter's dominions apparently extended from the Junk River in the east to a little river in the west, "about half way from Cape Mount."

"They Possess Genius, Think Justly, Speak Correctly"

Marchais described residents of the Cape area as "large ..., strong, and well proportioned." He said, "They possess genius, think justly, speak correctly, perfectly know their own interests."

The quality of people's relationships impressed the French captain. Their friendships were lasting, but he warned visitors from flirting with married women because the men were "very jealous."

Children were showered with **tender love**. For that reason, visitors gained the friendship of parents quickly by hugging their children and giving them cheap gifts. Marchais said many villages were "swarming with children," which he attributed to two factors: First, the practice of **polygamy**. Second, the fertility of local women.

The French visitor took detailed notes on local buildings. He described the houses as round and "very neat." Unlike the huts, kitchens were rectangular and elevated. One side, which faced away from the wind, was without a wall.

The posts of building were in a row and cemented together with "a kind of fat, red clay." Marchais described the mortar as "strong and durable," even "without any mixture of lime."

Gold and "Fine Redwood" For Sale

Farms were cultivated in a careful and orderly way. Marchais claimed sugar-canes, indigo, and cotton grew "without cultivation." Cows, sheep, goats and hogs were cheap, so they were probably plentiful. People worked hard, but not as often as he wished. Regarding goods of interest to Europeans, Marchais mentioned **gold**. But he wasn't sure if it was found locally or brought from elsewhere. In the area also were many "beautiful and valuable woods," including a "fine **redwood**."

The woods and waters surrounding the villages teemed with creatures — some beautiful, others useful, and a few threatening. Perched in the trees were a variety of colorful birds. The waterways yielded plenty of fish and turtles. On the grasslands, wild **deer** quietly grazed alongside the cattle. But three predatory animals lurked nearby.

Elephants were numerous. They rampaged through farms and damaged crops. When killed, they yielded meat and ivory. Leopards frequently attacked cows, other livestock, and sometimes people! Fruit trees were laden with delicious delicacies. But monkeys sometimes picked them quicker than the people.

Marchais claimed *Tawu* Peter gave Bushrod Island to him. He advocated the establishment of a **French colony** at Cape Mesurado with a fort on the hill where Monrovia now stands. The French government did not heed his recommendation.

According to Marchais, Cape Mesurado was not as depopulated by the slave trade as some parts of West Africa. But that was about to change. The removal of African captives, which began with Pedro de Sintra, would soon increase.

An Englishman Maps the Rivers

William Smith was a surveyor sent by the **Royal African Company** of England to map the coast and major rivers. He left England for Africa in August 1726 and returned a year later in September 1727. About 17 years after his return, he published his account of his voyage.

On December 29, 1726, Smith's ship anchored off Cape Mount. He stayed there for 4 days, but he did not go ashore. On January 4, 1727, his ship arrived off the coast of Cape Mesurado and though it remained there a day, no one approached the ship.

A day later the ship arrived at the Junk River. This time Smith went ashore. He returned to the ship in the evening without talking to anyone, although he saw some local people on the shore.

Sailing east, Smith visited the mouth of the River Cess where he charted the entrance of that river. He found the villagers courteous but shy of the English. Water and wood were collected for the ship, but food was scarce, except for rice and fowl. **Scarcity** and **suspicions** were probably rising due to the kidnapping of local people to be carried into slavery.

Smith continued to sail down the coast and arrived at "Cetra-Crue" on January 20. Here a canoe approached the ship and Smith visited the town the next day. The local meal consisted of boiled rice and palm oil. Smith noted that other foodstuffs were scarce except for malagueta spice and pineapples. From Setra Kru, Smith's ship sailed past Cape Palmas to the coast of present-day Côte d'Ivoire, and then on to the Gold Coast (present-day Ghana).

In the early 1700s, Europeans reduced the buying of African products, preferring to buy people. British, French, and Portuguese traders pushed Dutch slave buyers out of the more lucrative **Bight of Biafra** and **Bight of Benin** along the coast of present-day Nigeria. Around 1740, Dutch slave merchants turned to the Windward Coast instead. By 1750s, the trade in enslaved Africans exceeded that in ivory, gold and other African goods.

A Three-Legged Trade

European governments and merchants organized the nefarious buying of kidnapped Africans and provided most of the money and ships. African kidnappers and warlords supplied the captives. Rich buyers in the Americas sent some ships and goods, like **rum**, to pay for captives who worked until they died on plantations and in mines.

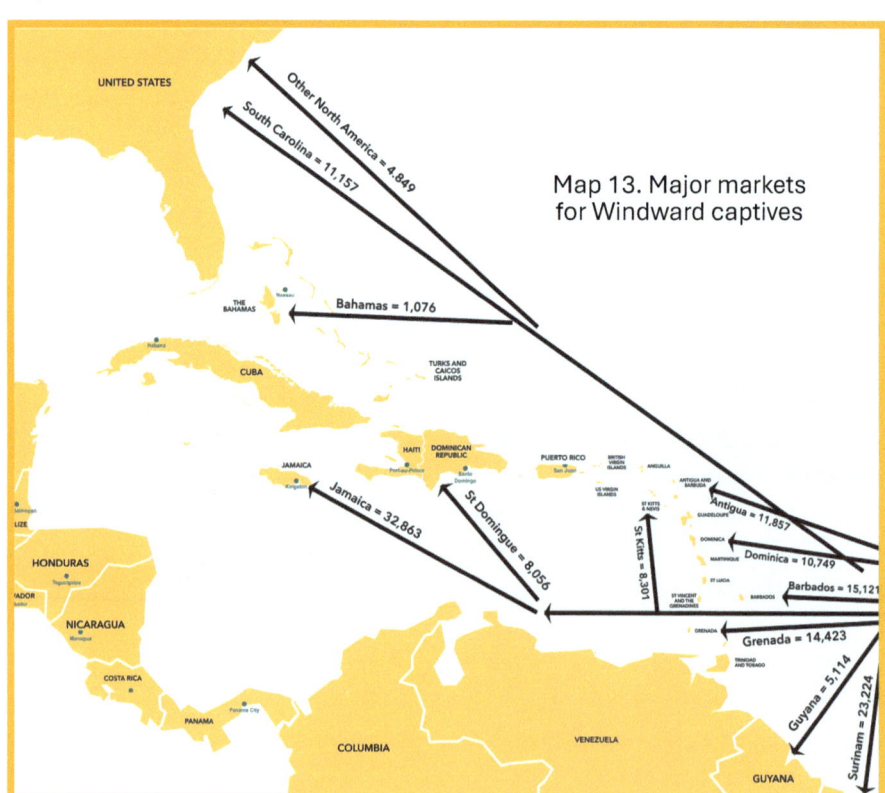

Map 13. Major markets for Windward captives

Because three regions of the world were involved in removing Africans, the business was sometimes called the **Triangular Trade**. It involved most European nations, along with their colonies in the Americas. The network got that name because it was shaped like a triangle. Linking this network together were Atlantic sea-routes between Europe, Africa, and the Americas.

Guns and Liquor for African Captives

Along the first leg of the triangle, ships carried manufactured goods to Africa where they were used to purchase enslaved Africans. European ships loaded with **guns**, **liquor** and other goods left ports such as **Liverpool**, **London**, and **Bristol** in England, **Nantes** in France, **Lisbon** in Portugal, and **Cadiz** in Spain. In Africa, European and American merchants exchanged cowrie shells, guns, gunpowder, gun shots, rum, cloth and brandy for African captives.

Except for Russia and the Balkan nations, most European nations were involved in buying and selling African **captives**. The major traffickers of Africans were Portugal, Great Britain and France.

The second leg of the Triangular Trade was called the **Middle Passage**. It involved ships travelling from Africa across the Atlantic Ocean to the colonies in North America, South America, and the Caribbean.

Their "cargo" were African captives tightly packed below the decks and chained to prevent them escaping. There they remained for most of the day.

A slave buyer inspecting a captive on the coast of present-day Liberia.

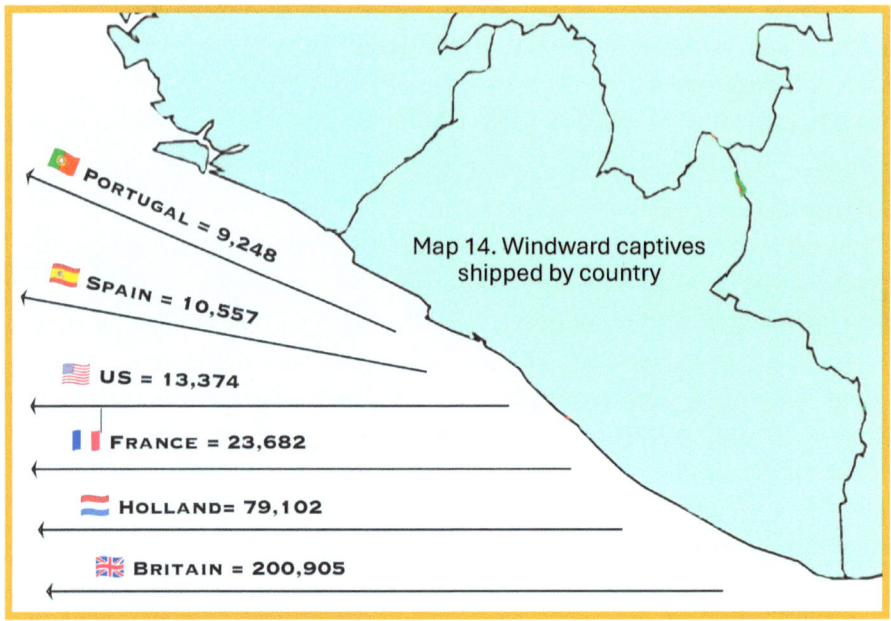

Map 14. Windward captives shipped by country

Little fresh air reached below the deck and the atmosphere was stifling, hot and smelly from sweat, excrement and urine. Another 1.8 million Africans died while crossing the Atlantic. Many died from despair, disease caused by unsanitary conditions, or punishment for resistance. Some in despair managed to escape their shackles and throw themselves overboard.

The third and final leg of the triangle was the journey of ships from the Americas to the ports in Europe. Ships came ladened with sugar, cotton, tobacco, and precious metals. The profit from these sales was then used to buy more goods to trade in Africa.

Enriching Europe and America

Scholars have assembled data from 34,948 trans-Atlantic voyages by slave ships. They estimate that approximately 40,380 voyages took an average of 265 persons each from Africa to the Americas.

Over time, the Dutch removed 16 percent of all their enslaved Africans from the **Windward Coas**t, more than from any other region. About 40 percent of all African captives sent to Dutch colonies in the Americas, including Surinam and **Guyana**, came from the area of Liberia.

In 1750, British slave buyers, mostly from Liverpool, overtook the Dutch. British participation peaked in the last quarter of the 1700s. They bought captives mainly from Bassa and Cape Mount.

As a result, the slave trade increased dramatically on the coast of what is now Liberia. That is likely why people at River Cess were suspicious of the English and food was scarce there. For the first time, slave ships began stopping regularly at places like Cape Mesurado, the Junk River, River Cess and Grandcess. But most captives were removed from Bassa, 23,374, and Cape Mount, 32,324. In the 1700s, more than 64,0000 kidnapped Africans were taken from the coast of present-day Liberia.

Local Lies About Kidnappings

Two **lies** about the slave trade have been popular in Liberia. The first lie says no Kru people were sold into slavery in the Americas. The second one says only criminals and war captives were sold from this region. Both of those claims are false, according to data from the highly reputable website called slaveyoyages.org. It shows that Kru-speaking people accounted for nearly a quarter of all West African captives carried by the Dutch to present-day Surinam as well as **Demerara** and **Essequibo** in present-day Guyana. Those captives from the Kru Coast were taken in the 1600s, during the time of the Quoja invasion.

The database also shows the ages and sex of the Windward captives were different from what many Liberians believe. More adult women than men were taken from this region. In addition, 40 percent of all captives were under the **age of 10**. Neither group fitted the profile of hardened **criminals**.

African Resistance to Slavery

Africans on both sides of the Atlantic resisted every aspect of the slave trade – from kidnapping, selling, and shipping to chattel slavery. Some committed suicide, while others refused to work, ran away, fought, **rebelled**, or campaigned for abolition. No matter the method, Africans demonstrated a fierce desire to be free.

A desire to return to Africa, also known as **repatriation**, emerged among captives as soon as they were removed from the continent. It persisted for hundreds of years among African descendants in scattered places, including Brazil, the Caribbean, North America and England.

At least 45 incidents of **resistance** to enslavement occurred aboard ships from the Windward Coast. These included four attacks by Africans from on land that prevented slave ships from leaving Africa. Between 1755 and 1761, one ship, the *Philadelphia*, captained by Jan Menkenveld faced three antislavery actions. They ranged from several captives jumping overboard to two insurrections.

The largest and most influential slave rebellion began in 1791. It was the **Haitian Revolution** led by **Toussaint L'Ouverture**. This revolt in the French colony of Saint-Domingue raged until 1804. During that time, all of the enslaved people were freed and many enslavers killed. Some former plantation owners fled to **Louisiana** and the **Chesapeake** region of the U.S.

One of the few anti-slavery actions that survives in oral history is the heroic story of **Vanja-Vanja**. He was a Gola man born in the **Dowo** Mountains of the Kongba region. He was reportedly large in stature with great strength.

Vanja-Vanja Fights Enslavers

On a visit to the Cape Mount coast, Vanja-Vanja saw many Gola children being loaded onto a slave ship. This incensed him so he decided to rescue the youths. He persuaded a friend to tie him up and sell him to the slaver on the pretext that he wanted to visit the "Whiteman's Country."

When Vanja-Vanja was on-board the slave ship, he saw that a large ferocious dog was being used to terrorize the captives. As soon as the ship had left land, he unleashed his plan. First, he seized the dog from the deck and threw it overboard. Next, he seized crewmembers and threw them overboard.

Having spared the ship's pilot, Vanja-Vanja forced him to the steer the ship back to the coast. Once there, he freed all the captives.

Africa's Heavy Loss

In 1787, Swedish industrialist **Carl B. Wadström** visited Cape Mesurado. Outraged by devastating scenes of slave trading, he became an **abolitionist**. In his diary, Wadström wrote: "It is a misery that passes imagination; no day or night passes without hearing **wailing cries** of someone being dragged away."

In 1818, the British began blocking slave ships from entering the markets that previously sold large numbers of captives. As a result, they turned to the Windward Coast. Its share of captives increased dramatically, until the mid 1800s.

From 1514 to 1866, about 12.5 to 15 million captives were removed from Africa. In addition, two to three million captives died in Africa during the raids on their communities or on the journey to the coast.

In the Americas and Caribbean, the plantation owners enjoyed the wealth derived from the free and hard work of the enslaved Africans who labored to produce rum, sugar, cotton, tobacco and rice.

The profits made many in Europe and the Americas very wealthy. In Europe, it benefited the merchants who engaged in the human trafficking, bankers who financed the trade, factory owners who made goods for the trade, factory workers whose pay came from the goods that were sold in Africa, and the ordinary people who invested in the human trafficking trade.

But Africa suffered a **heavy toll** due to the number of people lost. Kidnappings, captures and sales of people destroyed communities across Africa. They also caused untold suffering both to the captives and to the relatives they left behind. It **set back** the development of Africa for centuries.

Echoes of the Past in the Present

How does the past **impact** the present? Which things have stayed the same? How did some things **change**? Getting answers to those questions is one good reason to study history.

One of the long-lasting legacies of the past was the Way of the Ancestors. Their "way" were the rules originally set by them. Those ways became the foundation for morality, law, and religion. **Morality** was taught through proverbs, parables and folktales. For example, stories about Spider the Trickster warned against selfish and greedy behavior. The presence of those elements across West Africa suggest they date back to an ancient time, before languages and cultures separated.

Early West African ancestors in the north left behind more than 30,000 paintings, drawings, and carvings on rocks and in caves. Those rock **drawings** show people making music, worshiping, and wearing masks while dancing. Many of their masks and decorations look similar to cultures in the region thousands of years later.

Way of the Ancestors

From 1590 through the 1700s CE, the **respect** for ancestors shown by local people and pouring of **libations** were recorded by European visitors. In addition, several sacred local rituals also matched the Way of the Ancestor practices. The first involved a visit to town by a masked dancer known in the tradition as "the forest thing." A second was the rite that marked the elevation of girls to women. A third was a **wake** where food and drinks were served prior to a funeral. Fourth, loved ones were buried in clothes and in jewelry for their journey beyond.

Even some superficial cultural practices persisted for centuries. For example, blue woven cotton **robes** were worn by several rulers. Like now, mothers carried their **babies** on their backs. That led one visitor to opine that local mothers were "outstanding in their tender care for their infants." In 1666 CE, the uniquely Liberian greeting of clasping the elbow while **snapping fingers** was recorded for the first time.

But three styles faded in popularity over the years. For example, Atlantic-language groups no longer file their front teeth as a mark of beauty. In addition, very few men now plat their hair or wear a lot of jewelry, as some of their ancestors once did. Similarly, women on the Kru Coast rarely decorated their bodies with raised tattoos.

Migrations and Trading

Other changes were more radical. For example, people **moved** several times and over great distances! Starting around 6,000 BCE, people from the Sahel gradually moved east, west and south into the forests of West Africa. As people moved, the original Niger-Congo mother tongue **split** into hundreds of languages. Due to migrations, the ethnic groups of present-day Liberia are not exclusive to Liberia. Many extend into neighboring countries.

For more information, see these:

Adas, M. *Machines as the Measure of Men* (Ithaca, New York: Cornell University Press, (1989).

Amin, Samir. "Underdevelopment and dependence in Africa: Historical origin," *Journal of Peace Research*, 9 (June 1972): 105-119.

Blaut, J. M. "Fourteen Ninety-two" (pp. 1-63), in J. M. Blaut, ed., *1492: The Debate on Colonialism, Eurocentrism and History* (Trenton, NJ: Africa World Press, 1992).

Drake, St. Clair. "The responsibility of men of culture for destroying the 'hamitic myth'," *Presencé Africaine*, special issue (English language version), No. 24-25 (1959): 226-243.

Hoerder, Dirk. "Migrations" (pp. 269-287), in Jerry H. Bentley, ed., *The Oxford Handbook of World History* (Oxford: Oxford University Press, 2013).

Holsoe, Sven E. and Joseph J. Lauer, "Who are the Kran/Guéré and the Gio/Yacouba? Ethnic identifications along the Liberia-Ivory Coast border," *African Studies Review*, Vol. XIX, No. 1 (April 1976): 139-149.

Holt, Thomas C. "Explaining racism in American history" (pp. 107-119), in Anthony Molho and Gordon S. Wood, eds., *Imagined Histories: American Historians Interpret the Past* (Princeton, NJ: Princeton University Press, 1998.

Long, Edward. *History of Jamaica* (London: T. Lowndes,1774).

Seligman, Charles E. *The Races of Africa* (London: Butterworth, 1930).

Trouillot, Michel-Rolph. *Silencing the Past: Power and the Production of History* (Boston: Beacon Press, 1995).

Liberian Ancestors Before 1800

Despite the hardships of life in the forest belt, Liberian ancestors forged a way out of no way. Locally made **iron tools** assisted in farming. Four products of the forest area dramatically affected the history of West Africa: **kola** seeds, **malagueta** spice, **salt**, and **rice**. Those goods influenced the opening and closing of trade routes, the migration of language groups, and even the rise and fall of empires in the Sahel.

The successes of Liberian ancestors once **dazzled** outsiders. According to a European visitor, local blacksmiths made his dull tools sharper and stronger than they were when created. Prior to 1683 CE, the Dutch filled entire ships with local malagueta. Even in 1701 CE, it was still possible to buy enough rice on the coast of present-day Liberia to fill a ship.

Using wealth from **trading**, people living in the Sahel created several powerful states, known as empires. Some ancestors of Liberians were involved. From around 1230 CE to 1450 CE, three empires in West Africa dominated the region. They were **Ghana** (300-1077 CE), **Kaniaga** (1180-1213) and **Mali** (1235-1450).

Along with Islam, Middle Eastern traders brought the **Arabic language** to West Africa. Learning Arabic offered African merchants two advantages. First, Arabic gave them access to more **markets** because it was spoken from Spain through North Africa to Arabia. Second, it had a script that allowed the language to be **written**.

On the bottom is a drawing by **Pablo Picasso**, world-renowned artist. On the top is a Dan mask that inspired his drawing.

The angular style seen in this sculpture led to the European type of art called **Cubism**.

Invasions

After the collapse of the Mali Empire, five Mandinka "**war houses**" invaded the forest belt. They occupied areas around Kissidugu, Musadugu and Macenta in the west, Missadougou and Nzérékoré in the middle and Man in the east.

The next phase of the Mandinka expansion was known as the **Mane invasion**. It was apparently launched around 1560 CE. The leaders were able to recruit Mende, Bandi and Kissi fighters in their quest to wrest control of the European trade from coastal residents.

Before 1560 CE, 90 percent of the present-day Liberian forested land was uninhabited. The Mane pushed some ancestors of the Kissi, Loma, Mende, and Bandi over 100 miles south. The ancestors of the **Mende** traveled about 200 miles from their earlier location around Musadugu in Guinea to settle around Kenema in Sierra Leone. The people known as **Loko** in Sierra Leone are descendants of **Bandi** who accompanied the Mane. They moved almost 200 miles from the area north of **Foya** in Liberia. The **Gola** moved from Kongba, their homeland, closer to the coast.

Between 1614 and 1651 CE, the **Kamara clan** launched a major attack called the **Quoja invasion**. Starting from the Nzérékoré region in present-day Guinea, they targeted coastal and forest communities in present-day Liberia. The leaders of rival Quoja groups had Malinke names, like Manimassa and Mendino. This suggests many of the conflicts among them were family feuds. The desire to collect tribute motivated them, *not* ethnicity. Their power derived more from fear than respect.

These new invaders did not clear virgin land at first, as other groups had done. Instead, they seized control of key trading areas that were already occupied. Today, members of the Kamara clan live on land in both Liberia and around Macenta in the Republic of Guinea.

The **Quoja fighters** were probably paid mercenaries, who lacked ethnic or religious loyalty to Mandinka organizers of the invasion. As some Kpelle, Ma, and Dan were pushed south, they displaced **Kru speakers** from the edge of the savannah into the forest.

The conflicts between the Mandinka and the people of the forest were like other clashes between **empires** and **democratic** societies. When faced with a greater outside power, smaller societies either rallied together or faced certain defeat.

Arrival of Europeans

In 1462 CE, the first Europeans visited the area of present-day Liberia. After 1462 CE, Europeans increasingly developed a **direct trade** with societies on the coast of West Africa. By doing so, they achieved two long-held dreams. First, they reaped great wealth from malagueta, salt, gold and other goods. Second, they bypassed Muslim traders in North Africa and the Sahel who had previously served as middlemen.

By 1620, there were local rulers and traders on the coast who spoke Portuguese, French, or Dutch. In the 1700s, many rulers along the coast of present-day Liberia were called **Peter**, Pieta, or Pedro. That name would continue in use for many generations.

Lasting Harm, Pain and Shame

The slave trade mainly took away men and women in their prime. The forced removal of Africans caused untold **suffering** both to the captives and to the **relatives** they left behind. It set back the development of Africa for centuries. Their removal interrupted the flow of culture and **social values** from one generation to another. To make matters worse, captives were often exchanged for guns, which fueled more violence and **instability**. African rulers and merchants welcomed guns as a way to defeat their rivals. But wars disrupted mining, farming and peaceful living in Africa.

The slave trade also had a devastating impact on the Way of the Ancestors. Previously, it had served to preserve order, morality, and life itself. But kidnappers and sellers of captives subverted its purpose. They began convicting innocent people of "crimes" in order to sell them.

Western merchants in West Africa established a pattern of **unequal trade** that continues. They sold expensive finished products while mainly buying minerals and other **raw materials**. By selling gold, ivory and malagueta, Africans failed to promote local industries. In addition, importing guns, rum and other expensive goods made Africans poorer. In this trade, West Africans were the losers.

Racism in African History

One consequence of some Africans kidnapping and selling other Africans to Europeans was the development of racism. The term **racism** describes a system of thinking and behaving that assumes Europeans and their descendants are superior to other people, especially Africans. They portray themselves as heroes who must save the "primitive" and "savage" peoples of the "dark "continent of Africa. Racism affects how people write African history.

Similar to the Arab's selective use of the Quran, European and American slave traders used the **Bible** to justify slavery. Citing the Book of Genesis, they said Africans were ordained by God to be slaves. European and American slave owners, almost all of whom were Christians, said they were carrying out God's plan by buying and using Africans as slaves.

Racism on Display

Saartjie Baartman of South Africa was shipped to London in 1810, where she was forced to dance almost naked in public. Crowds of people came to see her and laugh at her butt. The top image shows a different Khoikhoi woman who was photographed for similar reasons. **Ota Benga** from the Congo (below) was displayed in a monkey cage at an animal zoo in the United States in 1906.

European visitors to the Windward Coast often offered insulting comments on customs they did not understand. Many words have two levels of meaning. One level is the literal or dictionary definition of a word. It called the **denotation**. The other level is the implied or suggested meaning. It is known as the **connotation**. The connotation of a word has favorable or unfavorable associations.

Many words with negative connotations have been used by Western writers to describe Africans. One example is Nicholas Villault who described ritual objects as "fetishes," meaning "false gods." Another is Jean Barbot who dismissed local Kru languages as "**barbarous**" and "utterly unintelligible."

After the Mane invasion, a Portuguese visitor wrote about some fighters eating their captives. He insisted that cannibalism was not normal in any local culture. In fact, invading troops terrorized people by eating human flesh only because it violated deep-seated local taboos. But later racist scholars would cite such behaviors as normal among Africans.

As a result of the slave trade, the world came to view Africans as stupid, **backwards** and **inferior** to other people. For example, several oral traditions mention the search for wild game to stories of migration. In truth, the ancestors of Liberians had lived settled lives until repeatedly uprooted by more powerful invaders. They routinely kept small animals for food,

Cobwebs of Isms and Schisms

Racism works like a **cobweb** to trap people who don't think for themselves. Since the 1970s, historians have paid close attention to the words used when about Africa. They try to use words that are **neutral** in meaning. Likewise, they avoid using words that insult an entire group of people, cast them in a negative light or blame all members of the group for the wrongdoing of a few. To do the same, always ask yourself four questions about history:

What do I *think*?
Why do I think that?
Where is the *proof* to support that way of thinking?
Is my source *biased*? For example, does he or she seem to praise or condemn an entire group of people?

But racists are not the only spiders spinning **dangerous** webs. We do the same thing anytime we portray all members of a group as criminal, ugly, backward or in any way less than us.

Sexism works the same way to keep women down. It portrays women as inferior to men and fit for only lower-level jobs.

Tribalism divides people, too. Tribalists assume that their ethnic group is superior to all others. When talking about an ethnic group besides their own, they will portray all members as ugly, evil, backward or criminals. They make such statements based on **bias** and "they say," not facts.

By choosing words carefully, you, too, can avoid racism, sexism or tribalism in your speaking or writing.

like chickens and goats. During their forced migrations, wild game would have provided their main source of protein. But many Western scholars assumed the people in those stories had never farmed, herded, or smelted metal. In their words, Liberian ancestors were "**primitive**."

Although not negative, some words used by European visitors were simply confusing. For example, they often referred to kingdoms in West Africa. But "kingdom" had more than one meaning in earlier times. They did not mean that local people were unified under a single ruler. Instead, they often used "kingdom" to describe people who shared similarities in language and culture.

Points to Ponder

Three deeper points from the past are worth remembering. First, people must tell their own stories using **the right words**. Words like "country devil" and "tribes," as well as insulting names like" Gio" "Belle," and "ex-slaves" must be banished. Their continued use fuel division and a sense of inferiority. Second, reading, writing and critical thinking are *essential* for progress. Throughout history, highly **literate societies** have outsmarted non-literate ones. Third, selling raw materials, whether kola, salt or gold, is a losing game. It keeps the sellers controlled by traders and the makers of **processed goods**. These three chains to perpetual poverty must be broken.

Credit for Images

Cover design, maps and interior book design by C. Patrick Burrowes

Kola plant: By Franz Eugen Köhler, Köhler's Medizinal-Pflanzen - List of Koehler Images, Public Domain, https://commons.wikimedia.org/w/index.php?curid=255532 .... Cover and p. 40

Salt in basket from Shutterstock, salt fields.. Cover and p. 40

Malagueta from Adolphus Ypey, *Vervolg ob de Avbeeldingen der artseny-gewassen met derzelver Nederduitsche en Latynsche beschryvingen*, Eersde Deel, 1813, tab 87 .... Cover and p. 40

Map of West Africa by Tom Patterson, US National Park Service national borders : File:NED worldmap 110m.svg by Gringerecoregion shape : File: Afrotropical biomes.svg by Terpsichores, CC BY-SA 3.0, https://commons.wikimedia.org/w/index.php?curid=23447200 22

A silk cotton tree, "Ghost lore: The value of Tobago's jumbie stories," *Trinidad and Tobago Newsday*, Nov. 12, 2020. 9

Storyteller from https://issuu.com/afrimissions/docs/7.4_hi-res. 12

Rock painting from Tassili n'Ajjer, Algeria,

https://commons.wikimedia.org/wiki/File:Afrikanischer_Maler_001.jpg 18

Photo of traditional acrobats, photograph by Michel Huet, 1950 28

Painting of Mami Wata, printed in the 1880s by the Adolph Friedlander Company in Hamburg, reprinted in 1955 by the Shree Ram Calendar Company in Bombay. 31

A helmet mask of the Sande society, 20th century, Sierra Leone, Mende peoples, wood, pigment, metal, height 16-1/4 in., wood-sculpture, the Met Museum, New York City 36

Blacksmiths at work from Arnold Ludwig, ed., *Ferdinand Hirt's geographische Bildertafeln : eine Ergänzung zu den Lehrbüchern der Geographie* (Breslau, Germany: F. Hirt, 1884), Vol. 1, p. 104 38

Pontan sculture from Bwoom-Gallery, Ernst-Moritz-Arndt Str. 171, 38304 Wolfenbüttel, Deutschland 53

Twisted iron bars from "Kissi money sticks," Schomburg Center for Research in Black Culture, Art and Artifacts Division, The New York Public Library. New York Public Library Digital Collections. https://digitalcollections.nypl.org/items/510d47db-b9b3-a3d9-e040-e00a18064a99.. 53

Cotton cloth from Baule African Textile, https://thenigerbend.com/products/

baule-african-cloth-textile-wrapper-53-x-43. 56

Caravan of porters crossing a river from Arnold Ludwig, ed., *Ferdinand Hirt's geographische Bildertafeln : eine Ergänzung zu den Lehrbüchern der Geographie* (Breslau, Germany: F. Hirt, 1884) 59

Donkeys in the Sahel, INTERFOTO / Alamy Stock Photo, purchased 24 April 2025..60

Camel caravan in the Sahara, "Camel Caravan in the Desert Sahara Morocco," Adobe Stock Images, downloaded 9 May 2025 61

Gold coins from "Hidden Histories: West African Gold" exhibition at Colchester+Ipswich Museums, https://colchester.cimuseums.org.uk/westafricangold/ 63

Ivory plaque, Dittico Queriniano in Museo di Santa Giulia (Brescia), public domain. 63

A map of West Africa drawn in 1375 CE by Abraham Cresques from Atlas de cartes marines, Bibliothèque nationale de France, Département des manuscrits, Espagnol 30. 68

Man standing in an archive, "'Badass Librarians' Foil al Qaeda, Save Ancient Manuscripts," *National Geographic*, https://www.nationalgeographic.com/history/article/badass-librarians-joshua-hammer-timbuktu-manuscript-al-qaeda 72

Great Mosque of Timbuktu, "A Tribute to Islam, Earthen but Transcendent" *The New York Times*,18 April 2012 75

A compass, writing quill and map from https://www.freepik.com/premium-photo/vintage-magnifying-glass-compass-goose-quill-pen-spyglass-lying-old-map_23149039.htm. 78

A Portuguese caravel from https://www.shutterstock.com/image-illustration/portuguese-caravel-fifteenth-century-computer-generated-183980678 81

Painting of Mandinka fighters on horses from "Wadai horsemen fighting against the French," *Le Petit Journal*, 5 February 1911..................................... 88

Sketch of Fula fighters from INTERFOTO / Alamy Stock Photo, purchased 24 April 2025..96

Civilians fleeing invaders, adopted from Arnold Ludwig, ed., *Ferdinand Hirt's geographische Bildertafeln : eine Ergänzung zu den Lehrbüchern der Geographie* (Breslau, Germany: F. Hirt, 1884), Vol. 1, p. ?? 100

A Dan power society mask from AfricaDirect.com... 105

Scene of Quoja country from P.E.H. Hair, Adam Jones, and Robin Law, eds., *Barbot on Guinea: The Writings of Jean Barbot on West Africa 1678-1712* (London: The Hakluyt Society, 1992), vol. 1, p. cxiii for details. 117

British and French ships fighting in 1798, unknown artist, "Scene of the Battle of the Nile, August 1798,". Wikimedia, ... 110

African ivory porters, wood engraving by Godefroy Durand for *The Graphic*, 30 October 1886...114

Drawing from Jean Barbot of his meeting with the ruler of River Cess, by engraver Johannes Kip from Jean Barbot book in *A Collection of Voyages and Travels*, Vol. V (London: John and Awnsham Churchill, 1744) ......107.

Bassa sculpture showing raised tattoos from Africa Direct shop, https://africadirect.com/products/bassa-divination-female-figure-scarification-liberia-122728 119

Rice bird nest from P.E.H. Hair, Adam Jones, and Robin Law, eds., *Barbot on Guinea: The Writings of Jean Barbot on West Africa 1678-1712* (London: The Hakluyt Society, 1992), vol. 1..120

African captives being lowering into the hold of a slave ship from: https://www.thoughtco.com/images-african-slavery-and-slave-trade-4122913 122

Cape Mesurado village from engraving by K. De Putter in book of Chevalier des Marchais 126

A slave buyer, engraving by Whitney, Jocelyn & Annin was originally published in *Captain Canot, or Twenty Years of an African Slaver* by Brantz Mayer...131

Painting by Pablo Picasso, "Head of a woman," 1907. 139

Dan mask that inspired Picasso, Picasso Museum, Paris, France................. 139

Photo of Saartjie Baartman of South Africa. "Hottentot woman" from a late 19th century newspaper, photograph signed Rudkert. 142

Ota Benga of the Congo, photographer unknown, 1906 photograph taken at Bronx Zoo, available at the Library of Congress. 142

www.ingramcontent.com/pod-product-compliance
Lightning Source LLC
Chambersburg PA
CBHW041619220426
43661CB00046B/1510